CLASSIFICATION: POETRY

A CIP catalogue record for this book is available from the British Library.

Printed and bound in Great Britain.

Cover photograph by courtesy of the North West Tourist Board.

This SOUTH EAST COUNTIES - London, Essex, Kent, Surrey and Sussex edition

ISBN 1-902803-55-8

First published in Great Britain in 2000 by
United Press Ltd
1 Yorke Street
Burnley
BB11 1HD
Tel: 01282 459533
Fax: 01282 412679
ISBN for complete set of volumes
1-902803-54-X
All Rights Reserved

www.upltd.co.uk

Straight from
the Heart

Foreword

What kind of world would it be without poetry? It would be a very cold place indeed - one missing a huge dimension that counts for so much on a planet where trivial things are often given so much unnecessary time and space. So many of us fill our lives with wasted hours in front of computer screens or TV sets. In the fast paced mayhem of modern life we human beings are becoming more and more like the machines we operate. We are all in danger of sacrificing our humanity to keep pace with our frantic technological lifestyle. But in this morass of madness come moments of poignant passion. And every time those moments do occur we should make sure we give them the time and space they deserve. Without them we are less than human. That is why poetry is so important. It allows us to express those deep emotions so clearly, to consider and analyse them and, ultimately to learn from them. Poetry can be an educational experience. It can teach us a lot about ourselves. So I hope that when you have read these pages you may learn something both about yourself and the people who have written these words that come - Straight from the Heart.

Peter Quinn, Editor

Contents

The poets who have contributed to this volume are listed below, along with the relevant page upon which their work can be found.

62	Yinka Agbetuyi	99	Natasha Bentley
63	Sylvia White	100	Barbara Davies
64	Cecilia Jane Skudder		Andy Tremayne
65	R N Taber	101	Len Spooner
66	Shaffick Hamuth	102	Janice Thornton
67	Miriam Bowman	103	Michelle Hurley
68	David Harris	104	Brian Marett
69	Gillian Tooth	105	David Woodcock
	Priscilla Westcott	106	Lucy Hunt
70	Yvonne Headington	107	Jan Wickens
71	Frederich Bathurst	108	Marion Durrant
72	Rebecca Kernick	109	Zoe Doyle
73	Shirley Hale		Leonard Wildman
74	Gavin Rodney	110	Sylvie Sorrell
75	Ann Sheridan	111	Sandi Evans
	Rosalind Wood	112	Hollie Salter
76	Mary Baird-Hammond		Yvonne Sparkes
77	Rachel Lyon	113	Peggy Wheeler
78	Josephine Idries	114	Susan Sparkes
79	Jennifer Jeffryes		Peggy Stoker
80	Julia Middleton	115	Sarah Bidgood
81	Michelle Singh	116	David Brookes
82	Jane Ault	117	Corinna Collins
83	R Limage Jones	118	Cynthia Berry
84	Allen Jessop	119	Laura Rydings
85	Amy Hagan		Gemma-Marie Crane
	Emma Knuckey	120	Andrew Humphrey
86	Urslin Constantine	121	Mary Simpson
87	Stella Elliott	122	Carrie Stonebridge
88	John Sharp	123	Elizabeth Smith
89	Audrey Wright	124	Jim Wilson
90	B Mooney	125	Nancy Johnson
	Robert Hallmann	126	Sonia Bowen
91	Lee Dohoo	127	Pamela Constantine
92	Jane Sagrott		Emma Keenan
92	Mick Nash	128	Michelle Read
93	Helen Gust	129	Marion P Webb
94	Stacey Wager		Verity Burgess
95	Susan White	130	Raffalina Peluso
96	Elaine Mumford	131	Nina McLeod
97	Jacqueline Harnett		Mary O'Keeffe
98	Hilary Robson	132	Jean Owen

133	Stephen Moles		Sarah Ridge
134	Ron Dean	165	James Critchley
135	Sue Sherriden	166	Frederick Seymour
136	Peter Bridgeman	167	Janice Walpole
137	Lorna Charles-Cross	168	Gwen McRandal
138	Kevin Worsnop	169	Paul Redrup
	Kim Reeves	170	Christine Bishop
139	Christina Palmer	171	Pat Sturgeon
140	James Parsons		Rita Laundon
141	Antoinette Christine	172	Nikki Wood
	Cox	173	Geraldine Foy
142	Milly Hatcher		Suzan Gumush
143	Daniel White	174	Cye Thomas
144	Kenneth Shepherd	175	Bill Stanley
	Clare Ball		Claire Miles
145	Betty Blythe	176	Tim Bratton
146	Shareena Eradhun		H Bryant
147	Sigrid Marceau	177	Eirlys Jones
148	Chloe Boswell	178	Maurice A Smith
149	John Hills	179	Juliette O'Brian
	Lydia Dunn	180	P M Mayfield
150	Caroline Candy		Katie Farrell
151	L R Sanders	181	Marian Rutland
152	Gillian Harris	182	Jane Evans
	Cheryl Murray	183	Herbert Smith
153	Ian Collaway		Nikki Law
	Carey Sellwood	184	Joan Cooke
154	Philip Woodrow	185	Jillian Hockley
	Keith F Lainton	186	Michael Robertson
155	D G Llewelyn	187	Annabel Kinnear
156	Sara Ring	188	Mildred Barney
157	Pam Coughlan	189	Trixie Bolter
	Ann Beard		Alison Lanning
158	Cynthia Dray	190	Montserrat Kidwell
159	Joy Sheridan	191	Valerie Ryan
160	Elizabeth Young	192	John Burstow
161	Tanya Stephens	193	Jean Fitzgerald
	H Rich		Anna Parkhurst
162	Jean Godfrey	194	Meri Gadd
	Patricia Dawson	195	Ronald Bailey
163	Mike Phelps	196	Jessica Jarlett
164	Nola B Small		Andrew Fleming

AGELESS CHARM

Beautiful once youthful
Youthful and graceful
Like a ballerina in Swan Lake
A ballroom dancer you were once

Beautiful once youthful
Age has withered
Death of a spouse
The anger you feel

Radiant in beauty
Your presence enhances
A psychic quality you bestow
A conventional wisdom you hold

Youthful and graceful
Age has withered
An elegant persona
A crippled poise
Shuffles in an arthritic gait

Joan Myrlin Celestin, Edmonton, London

To a very gracious lady, Margaret Wardale, my friend and inspiration. Happy 84th birthday Mags. Best wishes. Love, Joan.

Joan Celestin said: "I was born in Curacao, Northern Antilles of St Lucian parentage and grew up in St Lucia in the West Indies. I was employed by the Civil Service in Britain for 16 years but had to compulsorily give up work in 1997 due to a clinical accident. I appreciate art, photography and crafts. I took a Creative Writing course last Autumn and discovered that I could write poems. This is the first poetry competition I have entered and was surprised that one of my poems was selected to be amongst the showcase of the best work of other poets. Writing has provided an outlet as a source of therapy and healing art in being able to express my feelings and as a coping mechanism. My greatest ambition is to publish a book of my poems and drawings as a collection as they may provide some insight into self-healing by creative expression."

JUST A MEMORY

Part of my life slipped by with you
and now you're gone.
Now you're just a memory
of time we shared.
How can two people be so close,
mean so much,
then walk away?
We laughed at the same jokes,
planned the same plans;
working side by side,
we dreamed the same dreams,
And when we cried, we cried together.
We were as one.
Even the smell of you was second nature to me.
Now, there is nothing -
and all you are
is a smile at the end of a recollection.

Julie Holness, Tankerton, Whitstable, Kent

SLOW SUICIDE

You may have thought that it was big to have a little drag,
Or maybe it was just a sniff from a plastic bag.
Was it just a youthful fling to keep the boredom at bay,
Now the habit has increased, you'll end up dead, one day.

The standards that you set yourself have rapidly gone down,
You're living in a run down squat on the wrong side of town.
Your clothes are tattered and torn, your body's thin and
gray,
You've become a pushers pawn, you'll end up dead one day.

The men in blue called round today, to take me to the
morgue,
They'd found your body, in conditions unfit for a dog.
At first I said "That's not you, you never were that old"
But drugs had taken your youth away and left you lying

In the "Shooting Gallery", a junkies own Skid Row,
See them lying, dying there, they've nowhere else to go.
So ditch the Dragon, kick the Coke and throw glue aside,
Break the habit for you're committing... slow suicide.
A drug addict's no self respect, cos' snow blew his pride,
Losing hope, through using dope...it's slow suicide.

John Hebbs, Sittingbourne, Kent

John Hebbs, from Sittingbourne in Kent. said: "I consider myself primarily as a song writer whose first love is lyrics, I have been writing songs since the sixties, many of them poems set to music. 'Slow Suicide' started life nearly 20 years ago as an anti drug song. Many of my songs were written with a performer in mind, ironically 'Slow Suicide' was written in a style to suit Mick Jagger."

HEART IN HIS SIGHTS

Shot with a heart-shaped bullet
That's what the papers said
If only she had listened
To what was in her head

But her heart knew better
Told her head he was the one
She never saw him fire
That heart-shaped bullet from his gun

Love's death was slow and painful
He didn't stay until the end
He just left a lonely victim
With a broken heart to tend

Her broken heart soon mended
And the memories put behind
She'll know next time for romance
Do not seek and ye shall find

Gillian Morphy, Beckenham, Kent

ONE YEAR

Wind the nature puppeteer's wrath,
Has jerked the leaves upon the path,
And slid the waves around the bay,
And swooped the flocks as angels may.

While the sun's wild flare wakes all things,
By the summons of each bird that sings,
And fleets the stars from morning sky,
And runs the stream of dark ink dry.

Rest the world in winter's slumber,
Fall clear pearls in April's number,
And season's skies be fresh and new,
And trace the world in silver hue.

Sophie Horner, Colchester, Essex

FILM LOVE.

I want love like in Hollywood!
Perfect, ideal, full of good.
Can I really have it? Can I please?
Go on providence. Just one wheeze!
A little bit of Doris Day
If allowed, I would never stray
Again from cruel reality.
Will thee, you glowing fantasy
Come true? Just for little old me?
I will settle for nothing less
Than pure lies: that my mind caress.
This is why love darkens my sun
With nights of dismal nothingness.

James Postgate, Whitstable, Kent

DESPAIR

Drooped eyelids that have felt too much
The whites seem to take over
The pinprick pupils in retreat.

Warm bile takes possession of my intestine
- Melting and blending;
Caving my breasts inward
To form two stalactites hanging from my rib cage.

Heartbeat so slowed and irregular
- It tricks my mind.

The stomach - grated and raw
- Can only somersault in sympathy
There is no time to replenish its juices
Before the throat again commands it upwards.

The head bowed into stooped shoulders
That have no strength left.

The legs that have run too far
Now buckle the body to the pavement and say
"we've had enough..."

Leanne Burbridge, Enfield, Middlesex

Born in Sydney, Australia, **Leanne Burbridge** enjoys travelling.
"It seems as if I have always been writing poetry," she pointed out.
"It feels as if I have to write and create. It helps me sort things
out and put them in perspective. My work is influenced by raw
emotions and natural states and to me nothing is sacred." Aged
33 she is a proofreader, editor and writer for industry publications
and she has an ambition to write a good book. She is married to
Derek and they have one daughter, Kelsey. Leanne has a BA in
creative writing and communications. She has written poems and
short stories but this is the first time she has had one published.

THE ROOK

The rook glared with its big belly hanging loose
But firm and efficient
Its head moved in three separate motions
Left, Right and Centre.

It stalked the land
The territory his - no boundaries within the prairies
The straw colour surrounded his black bones
It fired up in his eyes.

From afar it was peaceful
We stopped the motor high up
Soaring we looked Left, Right and Centre
Never knowing what we turned our backs on.

Amy Gardner, London

*For Michael Folkes who believed in my poetry and for giving
me the continual support and advice I needed.*

OUR GARDEN

No snow came to our garden this year
Just falling rain, from clouds so near
Those bright cold days seem long ago
When steel blue skies gave cheeks aglow.
Jack Frost he came, leaving a trace
Of sparkling dewdrops, on carpets of lace
He also left a trail of tears
As bulbs got frozen, arousing fears
That Spring arriving would seem much duller
Without those flower beds of colour.

We like to watch the squirrel bury
Nuts placed out, then away they scurry
Hiding from view as birds fly past
Hoping each nut will not be their last,
When yellow and purple heads appear
The crocus tells us, Spring draws near
Winter's shortened dark cold days
Are moving fast through final phase
Slowly turning warm and brighter
The days much longer, evenings lighter.

C Goldsmith, Enfield, Middlesex

*Dedicated to my wife Sheila. Without her love and insight,
my work would never have seen the light of day.*

CYBERSOUND

Stranger of my dreams
Through your sound
I can touch the stars
I can stretch my vision
and be a god.

A cosmos of light
and love and warmth
invades my being.

I float in the firmament
with formless phantoms
The barriers are invisible
yet I feel the boundaries
deep within me.

I am contained in this
microcosm of creation.

I have been there
I feel safe.

Cynthia Barker, Richmond, Surrey

WHERE WERE YOU?

What's the good of a posy,
Now that I'm lying dead?
I would rather have had a visit
When I was alive, instead.

What's the good of a headstone,
To show I'm lying there?
When nobody knew and nobody cared
When I sat alone, in a chair.

Why are there people here crying?
They can't be crying for me.

When I was at home and sitting alone
Nobody did I see.

When I sat in that hospital chair
Slumped to one side, did anyone care?
Waiting for God to call me home
Never more, to be alone.

Iris Green, London

Born in London **Iris Green** started writing poetry in her late
teens. " I discovered that it was a way to express my inner-
most feelings," she explained. "My work is influenced by
everyday life and my style is free and spontaneous. I would
like to be remembered as a caring person." Aged 67 she is
retired and has an ambition to have a collection of her poems
published. She is married to Bill and they have two children.
"My biggest fantasy is to have a major windfall to enable me to
aid others less fortunate than myself and my worst nightmare
is to be without my family and friends," she said. Iris has
written several poems and had three of them published. Her
other hobbies include drawing and painting.

UPON RETURNING HOME

Were you with me there today?
One of our favourite trips-
A smiling policeman at the gate,
The long and rather hurried walk
To the first necessary port of call.
Then to refreshment and a chat
About the weather maybe - good or bad
We didn't seem to mind.

Were you with me there today?
The pond, the shrubs, the grasses tall,
And that secluded seat,
On three sides hedges neatly trimmed.
We talked again - just little things
We didn't seem to mind.
Yes, you were with me there today,
As you are each and every day.

Alan Sharp, Sutton, Surrey

Born in North London, **Alan Sharp** enjoys writing, painting
and genealogy. "I started writing poetry over 30 years ago,"
he said. "I have always loved the English language. My
work is influenced by Stephen Smith and others at Scola in
Sutton. My style is multifarious, depending on class
assignments. I would like to be remembered as someone
who keeps on trying." Aged 71 he is retired and has an
ambition to find someone interested in his "Diary of Lupin
Pooter", son of a famous nobody. He is a widower with one
son, Paul. "The people I would most like to meet are my
grandparents, to find out what they knew of our family his-
tory," he said.

WINTER MOTH

Pale moth coming at my window
On longest of cold nights, with eyes ablaze,
How are you here, fingering the pane,
Or dancing at the street-lamp in a maze;

Then in the winter
Hedge where nothings green,
Drawn to your wingless partner, to be seen
There on a dry twig, on a dead leaf,
Moved to an ecstasy beyond belief?

John Paul Sayer, London

LONDON

City of semi-dark and silent death,
Heaped footprints: her hungry breath
Anchors immigrants: her seductive walls,
With seasonable variations, call
Northern appetites: her night winks
On celibate suburbs: her day thinks
On confidential world affairs:
Her Sunday eye, indifferent, stares.

City of snow faces and snap fogs,
Crowded solitudes; of catalogues
Of ghosts of villages; a sea
Of broken dates and morning tea.
Tenants in their private prisons
Peer on shelved dreams and indecisions:
And burnt-out altars weep upon,
With dry tears, a crystal apron.

F G Ward, Harrow, London

EASTER

Eastertime is here again;
The loveliest time of the year.
Spring spreads her green mantle on hill
And plain
And new life is everywhere.

The churches and chapels are decked
In white
To greet the glorious morn.
And the people all congregate to the sight
Of the old world newly reborn.

We hear the blest message of eastertide
That we've heard so often before -
The resurrection of Christ who died
That sin might triumph no more.

Valerie Ann Luxton, London

MOMENT OF PEACE

To wake in the morning and the first sight I see,
Is the beauty of what makes the day,
The sun rising through a misty sea of rainbows.
I could be anywhere,
It doesn't really matter
For I would still see the same, feel the same
And be complete
At that moment I was nothing
But everything touched me.

Maxine Ellis, Stonebridge Park, London

VAMP

Time moves through the centuries with
an immortal soul. Constantly aware of the
changing atmosphere.
The past and the present etched forever in a darkness of
life,
Which he cannot be witness to all the time.
Shut out from the joy of eternal sunlight, and locked forev-
er in his own tormented and timeless being.

Karen Zena Roberts, South Greenford, London

TREES

When young, I knew a tree
Fresh to the world - like me,
Swaying slender, cool,
By a forest pool.
Two of a kind, we played;
I danced through breeze touched shade,
No thought of storm or ill,
World's dark or future's chill.

But life cut down
Pure heart, green crown.

And this is why,
When I see tall trees
Serene in age and beauty
Kissing a sunset sky,

I want to cry.

Dorothy L Garrard, Greenford, London

APPARENTLY AN ELEPHANT

I am apparently an elephant
Who tramples down the tangled brush
Preparing paths for others
So that they can fly through if they must

And perhaps they will not notice
That their pathway is cleared for them
And never give a thought for
Any grey ones gone before them

I'm occasionally resentful
Of the path that I am clearing
But it's fun to be an elephant
That's why I'm persevering.

Steve Doak, Finsbury Park, London

THE INN KEEPER

If only the innkeeper had known
The couple to whom he barred his door!
If only he heeded Joseph's moan,
And pitied Mary, so sick and sore!

If only he knew the prophecy,
If only he saw the guiding star;
If only he saw the wise men's glee
Would he have sent them to manger far?

I'm sure, and in no doubt whatever,
He would have given his own bed and room,
Embellished rich, with gold and silver,
Saulting babe and mother - shalom!

Welch Jeyaraj Balasingam, Lewisham, London

SHE GAVE MEDAL BACK

She waited for news
Waiting not her usual strength
Her mind has a world view
Country has as well
Her recent marriage disrupted by a different
Kind of consent
A KISS OR A KICK
He still able bodied
Shipped back
Further back
From oil
And sand
And pathos
Proof of bravery awarded
But
She gave the hindrance back

Timothy Wesley, London

I NEED

Please take your foot from out my face,
I need my own time and I need my own space,
I need to be left alone for a while,
I need to find a reason to smile.

Please let me take your hand in mine,
I need your light to help me shine,
I need your body to help my soul,
I need to feel that I'm in control.

Please do as I ask and not see this as greed,
So I can live the life I need.

Glen Byford, Enfield, Middlesex

CLEAR HEAD

Hackney born and bread
Went to Scotland to clear my head
All the things people said
Now I sit here on my bed
With many thoughts in my head
It all stands me in good stead
Cos I like butter on both sides of my bread.

Jay Pacer, London

DEAR ASHLEY WITH LOVE

From love to life is how you grew
The moment we met
Forever we knew
Tiny hands and tiny feet
Nine months on we were to meet
When I hold you in my arms
Forever I'll keep you safe from harm
I love you more and more each day
I sit and watch as you play
May God protect you from harms way
As I watch you grow from child to man
I know you'll do the best you can
I'm there forever to comfort you
To wipe your tears when you're feeling blue
To you I would give everything that I own
Never feel like you're ever alone
You are my world and I love you so
You lift my spirits if I'm feeling low
You are my son for that I'm glad
Dear Ashley with love to have you I'm proud.

Lorretta Fontaine, Tottenham, London

ACHIEVEMENT

How beautiful you are
Looking so elegant up in the sky
Delicately moving you cover the blue
This is your time to shine
Go ahead, take the centre spot
Revel in the attention you receive
Ignore the critics, don't feel the pain
When you are ready, let out the rain
Shower the earth with your toil
Scatter those gems without reservation
Take pride in your achievement
The fruits you leave will inspire
Your present will be appreciated
Your ability will colour the world.

T Bansel, East Ham, London

THE PRINCIPLE OF FAMILY

Virile and most indelible of social ties
Until one by one they all die
Values, experience dexterity ardently handed on.
For culture and social order must be won
Specified already whom shall inherit rights
Reform in power and status occur overnight
Services rendered
Decent sought and traced
Creating alliances
Waiting for those passed to be encased
The principle of the family
A complex ritualistic plight
Mutual obligations, economic organisation
A web of rights.

Shireen Pasha, Northolt, London

ARCHIVES

The whirring of the fan,
Soothing,
And appropriate.
Too much silence,
Welded
To the raucous violence
Of the noise of argument,
Discussion,
Discourse;
Encapsulated,
Enclosed,
In aged skin:
Holding words now,
Immortalised,
Where once
There was living sinew;
A being,
Destined to die.

Chander Bagga, Edmonton, London

MY HEART

My heart is split in two, because you've left me now
My minds sent trying to figure out, when why and how.
At first you said "it's love". You meant everything to me
My heart was under padlock, you had the only key.
It felt so good to hear your voice, that day on the phone
But you'd only called to say you were leaving me alone.
Was it for another girl? I don't know the reason why
As you hung up the receiver, I began to cry.
But through all my tears, I'd like to say to 'she'
I hope he'll never leave you hurt.
Because hurts how he's left me.

Scharrowne Khan, East Ham, London

JELLY-FISH

Spectral bodies surging in their May-time romp,
These translucent umbrellas hoisted in the sea
Trawling tendrils, undulating amidst the pomp,
Such deadly beauties, pulsing so majestically.

Polly Fleming-Wharram, Hampton, Middlesex

CHURCH CHOIR

Rehearsing for Christmas - the splendid church choir
keeping to standards that all would require.
The boss - his fingers flexed over keys with
positive verve and consummate ease,
Blessed with musical gifts and wit,
Harmony - four parts - directing to fit.
Oh no - not that old carol again.
Since when did you have the right to complain?
Chorister abashed used his vocals for song
Instead of his words sounding quite wrong.
Rebellion ran rife in the alto line,
We need to be heard with our notes so fine.
Sopranos turned round in a bit of a huff-
You can stop that big headed unnecessary stuff!
Tenors and basses - absolutely inflamed,
Our crochets and quavers - not to be shamed.
Thank you for your attention,
Words from the boss we must mention.
Back to "Dangerfield" - thank God,
But there's a danger in armchair to nod!

Thelma Bradbrooke, Harrow, Middlesex

JAMIE'S NIGHTMARE

Ghouls and ghosts and creepy things,
Screeching bats with outstretched wings.
Werewolves howling in the dead of the night,
Giving Jamie quite a fright.

Darkened graveyard with moonlit stones,
Skeletons rattling and shaking their bones.
Draculas fangs all dripping with blood,
Coffins and crypts and squelching mud.

With zombies rising from their graves,
Jamie with his cross feels brave.
But he wishes he was in bed tonight,
Under the covers, curled up tight.

But then he wakes to find he's home,
In his bedroom all alone.
It was just a bad, bad dream,
Then from under the bed - there comes a
                    SCREAM.

Linda Kersey, London

MARCH MORNING

Here the valley ends
With full, white curving drifts of snow,
Even now melting in the promise of sun,
The grass emerging,
Branches and brambles twinkling in light.
Here sheep wander and the small waterfowl
Breast the dark pond in arrowy flight.
Mournful, the wild geese mount high
With heavy wings cutting the dawn sky.

The March day grows,
Mirrored in water of the drowned fields,
Reflecting crystal and rose.
Light widens, spreads. The dumb sheep pause,
Sensing an indefinable, clean new air
As the dawn wind blows.

Peggy Denton, Upper Norwood, London

MISTLETOE

You bounce, you are my little tigger
Rubbing my nose in Eskimo kiss
Fidgeting, jumping, pushing into my hand
I have an irresistible urge to hug you.
You want to be loved, that is all.
To live to be loved,
Do they give you enough?
Can anyone stroke you enough?
Total faith, you will always come back
In faith and hope you are free
The dark will never become you.

Ellen Ware, Brixton, London

INFINITE LOVE

When first he came he was so small
Hardly any size at all
With big brown eyes he looked at me
I wondered just what he could see.
Warm and soft within my arms
I was lost to all his charms.
I loved him from the very start
He completely stole my heart.

As he grew we formed a bond
To every word he would respond
He was always at my side
My protector and my guide.
For fourteen years he was my friend
And I was with him at the end.
You'll understand how much I cried
Took one last breath - and died.

Connie Levene, Wembley, London

FOUR LEGS AND...

You were my life
My silent friend
Loyal to the tragic end.
Who? What can replace
The wet nose nuzzle,
Those searching eyes,
After a days end walk.
Beneath evening skies
Or dawning hues.
Rain, hail or frost
You ran by my side,
Then patiently when
Alone, you would lounge
Upon settee with paw,
Laid gently on my hand.
There are no words that
Can express, your sudden
Loss except, Adieu dear
Friend, rest in peace,
My noble guardian Tansey.

H A Brawn-Meek, Enfield, Middlesex

PEACE

All solutions
Have been dissolved

I realise
Things can never be solved

As all efforts
Are in an eternal hold

And left unsolved.

Nathaniel Gabriel-Lovell, London

MIR

It turns as slowly as a spit in space,
Nearly done

Still catching the sun
With the intelligence of ice.

A billion glacial particles
Glint in sequence

Compensating by calculation,
A minute shift in orbit.

It spills refraction,
Like a gunshot through the optics.

An accidental beauty, divined
From the gleaming geometry

Of mere science

Christopher James, Islington, London

OVER THE HILL

Creaking hips
Failing sight
Memory slips
Sleepless night
But
Long days
No tension
Patience pays
I've earned my pension.

S Lee, London

AT LAST

It was a cold, wet and miserable day
I looked through the rain soaked window pane
There was no sign of the sun
Why don't the clouds go away?

I don't like this terrible weather
So I'm going to bed to read my book
In the hope that it will make me sleep soundly
On my pillow of goose down & feather

I momentarily closed my eyes
And opened them with a start
When I heard a dog barking
And the sound of a cats' cries

The day had arrived without my knowing
And the sun was beaming in
Another day at last
Another day with the sun now showing.

Paul Tully, Islington, London

MORNING ROAD TO NESNA

Every pool is a dark reflection,
Autumn clinging to aspens, larches,
Rain lashing down on puddled meadows
Green and silent at early morning.

Mountains curtained by shrouded rainstorms,
Grass-etched roadways in russet shading,
Slender birch-trees are white as ghost-trees,
Pale as snow on the flat-topped mountains.

Fjords glisten from filtered daylight.
Sun emerges, metals the highway.
Water spouts over craggy outcrops.
Streams are ribboned in narrow gulleys.
Rivers cascade with organ thunder.

Cobalt blue are approaching fjords.
Midnight blue their surrounding mountains,
Hugla, Tomma and Handnesoya,
Forest-brown islands on storm-tossed waters.

Curving downwards the highway flattens;
Soon the turn off announcing Nesna.

Beryl Cross, Gunnersbury, London

VALENTINE

It's Valentine's day
And I am here to say
I love you loads
On this special day.

You're in my heart
I know we won't part
We was ment to be
Right from the start.

With gifts and cards
We give each other
The smile we show
There ain't no other.

The love we have
Is well in twine
Now I've got you
You're all mine.

Miss B McKeown, Enfield, Middlesex

AFTER A ONE NIGHT STAND WHO LEFT BEFORE MORNING

I dreamt of my shining crop of eggs
thought your team no longer there

Slept full of your dying dregs
was through moontime unaware

Woke with the fittest of your shoal
floating victory in my space

In the oval of the toilet bowl
saw my morning face

Flung the world from my oval mouth
the bottles and cats and sick surprises

Am now at battle with my oval mouth
until it brings me roses

Lucy Collins Ronowicz, London

ELSIE

Elsie moved when the blocks first went up.
An original tenant, with commemorative cup
From the G.L.C showing, stage by stage,
How slab met slab in the concrete age.

"It's not same now," she always complains.
"They've still not been 'round about those drains."
"When I first moved in, you could go out at night."
"Now just look at the rubbish, what a horrible sight."

Elsie never misses a single Town meeting.
Always there early to get the best seating.
She waits for her neighbours and then, when she's sure,
She raises her hand and takes to the floor.

A local celeb', with her blue rinse hair,
She tells us of times before we were there.
When children ran errands and people were kind
And thugs were locked up, not scolded or fined.

The Town Chairman sighs, as she must have her say,
Until others raise hands and she has to give way.
And so with a bow, she sits hands in her lap
And smiles to herself as we give her a clap.

Susan Wheatley, Thamesmead, London

FUTURE'S BRIGHT

The softness of your skin
Floating in ecstasy
When half my soul you took
Sensitivity heightened
Feeling enlightened
Golden light rushing through my veins
Feeling no pain
My life no longer so insane

Clarity is dawning
Wake up and stop yawning
Time to start something new
Future's bright, orange light
Inspiration in the air
Living life without a care
No more nine to five
I want to come alive

My time my own
No boundaries
No bondage's
Freedom to decide
No more need to hide

Dianna Bonner, Chiswick, London

SNOW

While flakes, softly falling
On the snow-white fleecy ground
Where everyone is calling,
There; the children playing around.

To see their tiny faces shine
Brings joy to all mankind.
Where footsteps they make
Fill up with snowflakes.

Their feet crunch through mountains of snow
Where a snowman big and round grows.
A hat, scarf, pipe and walking stick
Brings life to snowman Nick.

Anne Marie McHarg, Wembley, London

PAST CARING

War and famine
Maimed and emaciated
Spectres march through the living room.
News bulletins
New disasters
Ethiopia - Uganda
Bosnia - Rwanda
Vie for top billing.
Ethnic cleansing
Sectarian revenge
A computer game
Of virtual reality
Never quite taking us there.
Our saturated senses
Ooze and leak.
Compassion, sympathy
Are of the moment
Overwritten in memory
As advertisements take over prime time.

Bertha Newbery, Harrow, Middlesex

CITY LIGHTS

The sea is blue,
It gitters and sparkles
In the sunlight.

Boats to and fro
Who knows where they go
In the sunlight.

Cars cross the bridge
From north to south
In the sunlight.

The city awaits
The shoppers who stream
In the sunlight.

The night descends
And lights twinkle
In the darkness.

Mrs E A South, Wimbledon, London

MODERN LIFE

I'm so busy
I'm too busy too care
I'm just too busy to pray
I'm too busy to go to church
I'm too busy to worry about the poor
I'm just too busy to worry about crime
I'm just too busy to think about child abuse
I'm just too busy to sleep properly
I'm just too busy to think about the homeless
I'm just too busy to think humanity
I'm just too busy to have a holiday
I'm just too busy to bath properly
I'm just too busy to eat properly
I'm just too busy trying to make money.

Tony Wolliston, Leyton, London

I GAVE MY WIFE TO OXFAM

I gave my wife to Oxfam.
They said it was not so easy getting rid of the older model,
But they'd give it a try.
Had I noticed this one had a chip on the brain?
I know, I said, that's why I'm looking for another.
Not so easy to find a young Anglo-Saxon one, they said.
What about a 34 year old Albanian peasant at half price?
I'll think about it, I said.
I'll have a look around first.
Be back later.
Good luck, they said.
Don't worry about your wife,
If she doesn't sell we'll put her through the shredder
To make mattress covers for Romanian orphans.
She'd like that, I said.

Nancy Williams, London

THIS LIFE

I'm dying.
Red patches of skin eating my core away.
I fear for my new one,
It kicks as a portrait of my fear.

I do not want to be recognised when I die.
I have contributed nothing to the world,
But
This short note.

The woman died.
The child died.
And so did the flowers around the coffin.

Jolyn Andree Soo-Ling Lee, Edmonton, London

PEOPLE IN THE SKY

There are people in the sky tonight
Sitting together, quite still, floating
Through the air
High, high overhead
Inside their huge, robot bird
That cannot flap it's heavy wings
What a wonder!
Quite quiet... - Or you may catch it's hum
Like a droning bee,
Then, soundlessly once more,
Drifting through the vault, with twinkling lights
To mark it's passage.
It must be magic.

Robert Donald, Wembley, London

OLD LOVE

I want to run and chase you through the house,
Then when I catch you kiss and fondle,
And watch you throw your head back joyously,
As you laugh and sink onto the floor.
And I ask 'Where is my sense at 64.....?'

I want to make love wild and free,
Our moaning cries awake our envious neighbours
Then rest a little and begin again.
And as I count the score,
I wonder, are those the things one does at 64....?

Desire lies within your eyes,
As I run my fingers through your hair,
My longing for you never dies,
For you're still as perfect as you were before,
And I know that life is rich at 64.

Anne Grater, London

THANK YOU

You held my body on the day I was born,
You held my hand when first I learned to walk,
You made me smile when I started to cry,
Cleaned my wounds, fed me and kept me warm.
Walked me to school and watched me grow,
You were there when others let me down.
For the joys and sorrow I gave to you,
I say thank you for being my
MOM

Patrick Dacosta, Clapton, London

THE EXPERIENCE OF SHOPPING

Many of the shops I visit the style of fashion some stores do lack
The colours are mainly black, brown and grey
I like to purchase a garment which looks the price
To find that special garment I have to look twice

Little I know that store consists of an open changing room
I hope I don't walk out with that facial expression of gloom
Often I like more than one garment resulting to me making a compromise
Other days it's difficult to find my size

Here I go with a size fourteen through that embarrassment moment again
In the mirror I see the reflection of other skinny women with a size ten
I concentrate on trying on the garment those skinny images I must Ignore
My confidence is lacking quickly even though I have done this task before.

Carmel, Wembley, London

ACROSS THE MILES

The telephone rings
A friend
Ringing to find out how I am.

Listening to your voice
I feel a smile in my heart
So glad to know you are alright.

I want to put my arms around you
To tell you that I love you.
The distance between us
Has been covered.
I picture you and me face to face.

Your love is fragile and precious
To me.
You are in my heart
And I want you to stay there.

Eva Young, Tottenham Green, London

DEAD OAK TREE

It is the huge sheer drama of an elephant's foot
Planted mightily upon the earth.

Primitive, maybe even a dinosaur.
It is dead now, has been dead for years.

Yet I sense the majesty of it's former glory
Ghostly, it has a presence still.

It has been left, respectfully
And birds still alight upon it,
And I look and marvel
At this total new-age totem pole.

The resonance fills the nearby air.

Sarah Guppy, Southgate, London

"I started writing poetry to make sense of an often crazy
and inhumane world," said **Sarah Guppy** who was born in
London. "My style is influenced by nature, nature, Keats
and nature and I would describe my style as individual. I
would like to be remembered as someone who wanted to
share her light, experiences and insights." Aged 34 she is
a customer services advisor with an ambition to save the
world from ecological destruction. "The person I would
most like to meet is Kofi Annan from the United Nations,"
she said. "He is a kind of guardian of the globe and
nobody knows it." Sarah has written many poems and had
several of them published. Her hobbies include thinking,
reading and swimming.

DID YOU EVER DARE

Did you ever dare
To climb the highest fence
Or jump over a four foot wall
Scale to the top of a big oak tree.

Did you ever dare
To swim out to the middle of the pond
Jump down six stairs at a time
Or run across a busy road.

Did you ever dare
To kiss a boy under the backroom stairs
Enter into the footballer's changing rooms
Or colour your hair different shades of blue.

I did!

Catherine Sweeney, London

Born in London **Catherine Sweeney** enjoys reading writing
and music. "I started writing poetry around 1986 during
the illness of both my parents who died of cancer,"
explained Catherine. "My work is influenced by everyday
life and I write from the heart. I would like to be remem-
bered as a compassionate and humane person." Catherine
is a civil servant with an ambition to have some of her work
published. She is married to John and they have four chil-
dren. "The person I would most like to meet is Nelson
Mandela because he has great strength, which I admire
very much," said Catherine. "The person I would most like
to be for a day is a millionaire." Catherine has written
many poems but this is the first time she has had one pub-
lished.

TRAMP

Matted mane,
Broken trainers,
Charred, cheap trousers

A thousand rough
Nights etched
Into an atlas
Of engrained wrinkles;
Every road a story.

Tramp, vagabond,
Gypsy, knight
Of the road.

Body wracked with
Hacking cough;
Puffed, suppurating leg
Ulcers oozing wetly;
Pain his only friend.

Living dead!
Some nameless
Woman's beloved son.

Dave Fanshawe, London

LONELINESS

Loneliness is a tear stained pillow in a night of empty dreams.
Loneliness is a sudden end to a thousand
romantic schemes.
Loneliness is that old man who lives there on his own.
Loneliness is knowing your a thousand miles from home.
Loneliness can be in a crowd or in an empty room.
Loneliness is an emotion that fills the heart with gloom.
Loneliness is that empty feeling when someone has gone
away.
Loneliness is emptiness at the end of an empty day.
Loneliness is an empty place where someone used to be.
Loneliness is a piece of land far across the sea.
Loneliness can be for a moment or till the end of time.
Loneliness is for someone else, or it could be mine.

Bernard Tucker, Rotherhithe, London

"I worked in a monumental masonry business from the age of 15 until I went into the army and the inscriptions on the stones inspired me to write poetry," explained **Bernard Tucker** who was born in London. "My work is influenced by people, love and life and my style is emotional. I would like to be remembered as a good husband, father and grandad as well as a poet and visionary." Aged 69 he is retired and has an ambition enjoy his family and travel. He is married to Joyce Mabel and they have two children. Bernard has written hundreds of poems and had three published - one on video. "My biggest fantasy is to win the lottery and my worst nightmare is to wake up and find that it was a dream," he added.

POINSETTIA

Scarlet are her leaves,
Blood drops dripping,
Wounds of wantoness
Turned to awakening...

Autumn colours, comfortingly
Showing their maturity.
Paintings, alluring in their hue,
Summoning my spirits anew.

We wine and dine, toast
Various achievements,
Renewal of friendships
That time shall not sour.

Carol Plummer, Wimbledon, London

Born in Hatfield, **Carol Plummer** enjoys reading and Israeli
dancing. "I started writing poetry in 1997 in a creative
writing class," she pointed out. "I felt the need to express
myself literally and artistically. I have always been fasci-
nated by words. My work is influenced by DH Lawrence,
the poet Lotte Kramer and Shakespeare's sonnets and I
would like to be remembered as a poet and a performer."
Aged 56 she is an Israeli dance tutor with an ambition be a
recognised poet. She is married to Philip John and the
person she would most like to be for a day is the ballerina
Darcy Bussell. "The person I would most like to meet is Dr
Anthony Clare," she remarked. "I admire his ability to help
people understand themselves."

ICE FACE

Ice face
Wind-razed-remote
Nostril-sharp-sculpted slope
Repels glances
Eyes bounce back
Shocked. Lash-barred
Shutter drops a
Moment. Thin chills
Ache lips
The pass is closed.

Christine Shearman, London

Born in Barking, **Christine Shearman** enjoys reading and gardening. "I started writing poetry in the 1960's because I needed to let my heart speak," she remarked. "My work is influenced by personal experience and other poets and my style is modern. I would like to be remembered as a person who spoke her own truth." Aged 60 she is a psychotherapist with an ambition to write more poetry and a novel. She is divorced with two sons and has written around a 100 poems. "I have had about five poems published and I have also written articles," she said. "My biggest fantasy is that I may be granted health and time to write what I need to."

NEVER NEVER LOVE

YOu speak and your words remain suspended in air,
A new dimension created for words which have no mean-
ing,
A place where lingers everything I should have said but
didn't,
And every word I want to say but can't,
Instead your lips touch mine,
And a new language is spoken,
I am transported,
I dissolve like foam,
On a tidal wave of dreams I'll never dream,
Lives we'll never live
Children we won't have,
And time I can never recapture.

Emma Comolli, Winchmore Hill, London,

"I started writing poems and developed an interest in litera-
ture when I was at junior school. It was a way of express-
ing my emotions and feelings," said **Emma Comolli** who
was born in Hertfordshire. "My poetry is influenced by life
experiences, song lyrics, dreams and the work of other
poets. My style is romantic and introspective. I would like
to be remembered as a person who used the power of
words to transcend the boundaries of class, age, and gen-
der to speak directly to the human heart." Aged 26 she is
an advertising sales executive with an ambition to become
a successful writer and cabaret singer. "I have written over
30 poems but this is the first time I have had one pub-
lished," she said. "I have also written two short stories and
I am in the process of researching a novel."

I LIVE IN HOPE

I live in hope for world peace
To pray together for wars to cease
No more hunger suffering and pain
And for arid countries plenty of rain
To find a cure for illness that kills
And not having to take so many pills
To grow old with pleasure and grace
And for all the homeless a living place
I live in hope and also pray
For a better future to pave the way

Marie Wilkinson, Mile End, London

I dedicate this poem to Capi Harrigan because she cared and gave me good advice when I was ill, and she made me smile.

Born in Paddington, **Marie Wilkinson** enjoys writing and charity work. "My work is influenced by things that happen in my life and the world and I write with feelings and from the heart," she said. "I would like to be remembered by my writing and the fact that I was able to help people less fortunate than myself." Aged 41 she is a waitress with ambitions to help sick children and to have a book of her work published. She is married to David and they have one child. "The person I would most like to meet is Eric Clapton because I admire him and he has been through a lot," said Marie. "If I could be anyone for a day it would have to be Celine Dion, so that I could sing my songs."

RETIREMENT

When you come to the end of your working life
(It's the third age so I'm told)
Not the end of the road, I'll make it clear
But a chance to dig for gold.
So many hours are swallowed up
In the bid to earn a crust,
So many talents lie innate,
So many brain cells rust.
So now's the time to pause awhile
And set yourself a goal,

To join in things you really like,
And find your very soul,
To paint, to write, to sing, to act
Oh what an endless list,
There's so much chance for all of us
To catch up where we've missed.
So don't sit in that old armchair,
Forget about T.V
Discover what you want to do.
And jump in fearlessly!

Joan Leahy, Blackheath, London

SERVICE 109

I hate the bus -
It's all fuss.
Stopping and starting;
All congestion, no departing.
A mobile phone - bloody hell,
Next it will be the bell.
Too much graffiti on this upper deck -
It really is a pain in the neck.
Litter and grime, so little sunshine.
Misbehaving people, very loud -
That's the attention-seeking crowd.
horrible smells,
No deodorant - it tells
No conductor here,
Adding to the fear:
I hate the bus
In this London rush.

Lee McLaughlin, Streatham, London

Lee McLaughlin, author of "Service 109" is 35, and
Scottish. He now lives in Streatham, South London. Lee
has been writing poems for one year, and attends two cre-
ative workshops run for homeless people. He has produced
over 20 poems to date, mainly about towns and cities
around the United Kingdom. Lee said: "I have also penned
a number of political poems about homelessness and envi-
ronmental issues. I keep my work simple and honest, so
that all children can understand every word." Recently
three of his poems were displayed in Upper Norwood
Library, (Crystal Palace), London.

NAUGHTY BOYS

Good little boys are sunshine,
Bad little boys are not.
For naughty boys,
They get no toys,
They get what they have got.

Good little boys are delightful,
Bad little boys are not quite.
For good little boys,
Get a glass of milk,
And a story late at night.

Good little boys are wonderful,
Bad little boys are too!.
But naughty boys,
Get one hug and a kiss,
And good boys get a few.

So what's the difference between them,
I say there is not one.
Because both of them are beautiful.
And they both make my son.

Lucy-Anne Ball, Putney, London

Born in South West London, **Lucy-Anne Ball** enjoys writing, music, acting and playing with her son. "I started writing poetry when I was about 15 to express my feelings and emotions in a creative way," she explained. "My work is influenced by everyday life and my style is autobiographical. I would like to be remembered as a good, kind, reliable person who is strong and a loving mother, daughter and sister." Aged 19 she is a full-time mother with an ambition to be a professional writer of poetry or screenplays or an actress. "The person I would most like to be for a day is my son Toby, because he's so carefree," she said. She has written over 60 poems and had three published. She has also written a play and several short stories.

VALENTINE

It's Valentine's day
And I am here to say
I love you loads
On this special day.

You're in my heart
I know we won't part
We was ment to be
Right from the start.

With gifts and cards
We give each other
The smile we show
There ain't no other.

The love we have
Is well in twine
Now I've got you
You're all mine.

Miss B McKeown, Enfield, Middlesex

ONLINE

Just as the strife was won
To breach the line
Came another ploy to
Whip into line
Even as our tones refused
To toe the line
Our thoughts they sought
To trail online.

Yinka Agbetuyi, London

Born in London **Yinka Agbetuyi** enjoys writing and playing
tennis. "I started writing poetry 20 years ago," he said. "I
like to share my experience with others. My work is influ-
enced by Yoruba mythology and my style is lyrical and
engaging. I would like to be remembered as one who
helped make the world a better place through the power of
the word." Aged 41 he is a lecturer with an ambition to live
life to its fullest. He is married to Kehinde and they have
three children. "I have written over 50 poems and had a
few of them published," he said. "I have also written short
stories."

THE QUEEN MOTHER

The Queen Mother is a great lady,
One hundred years today
And the mother of our Queen,
Who's loved in every way.

Her looks are so impeccable,
Just like a treasured doll,
Sometimes appears to go out
For a slowly lingering stroll.

Some people wait for a glimpse
And hope she will appear,
This lady acknowledges the public,
Who wave their flags and cheer.

Every-one is pleased for her,
To see she is out and about,
A smile is always on her face
And you never hear her shout.

Sylvia White, North Cheam, London

Born in Battersea **Sylvia White** enjoys cooking, shopping
and sewing. "The first poem I wrote was 18 years ago
about my dog," she said. "I didn't write again until five
years ago when I lost my boy. My work is influenced by
what happens in life and I would like to think that my style
is pleasing to people and true to life. I would like to be
remembered for being kind and making people laugh. I like
to make people happy and I love children," Aged 67 she is
retired and has an ambition to write a book. She is mar-
ried to Donald and they have two children and 14 grand-
children. Sylvia has written over 50 poems but this is the
second time she has had one published.

STICKS AND STONES

Sticks and stones....
"Sticks and stones may break my bones, but words will
never hurt me."

We all know the saying often quoted when one's hurt.
When someone's spoken harshly with words that are so
curt.
How glibly do those words roll right off the tongue,
Even though the caustic has tears of anguish wrung.
Bruises from a beating soon fade and go away.
Memory of the feeling eases day by day.
But words can be so bitter, striking at our core,
Devastating lives and causing much furore.
The anger and the heartache may lead to many tears,
And lead to ruination of relationships for years.
Idle chitter chatter even if it's truth,
Can cause another hardship even without proof.
Still must our tongues be, whilst for guidance we do pray,
For when we slur another, 'tis Jesus hurt that day.

Cecilia Jane Skudder, Penge, London

Born in Dewsbury in Yorkshire **Cecilia Skudder** enjoys bad-
minton, tap and modern dancing, as well as writing poetry for
church newsletters. "I started writing poetry after my daughter's
mother in law died from cancer in 1997," she explained. "I wrote
a bereavement poem for her husband and I have written others
for people I have known in my work." Aged 55 she is a retired
Macmillan nurse with an ambition to be a good citizen, wife,
mother and grandmother. She is married to Bob and they have a
son and a daughter. "I have written over 100 poems and I have
been lucky enough to have had several of them published," she
said. "I have also written a journal of my grandchildren's early
years." when we asked her what her biggest fantasy was she
replied: "To be size 10!"

ASPECTS OF ECOLOGY

Flowers in the garden
Looking pretty;
Bees making honey
At the hive;
Kids in class, learning
About life.

Daisies on the lawn
Mowed down;
Queen bee robbed
Blind;
Out of sight, out
Of mind.

R N Taber, London

R N Taber said: "I was born in Kent and graduated from
the University of Kent in Canterbury, 1973. A librarian, I
now live in London. Some 200 of my poems have appeared
in various UK and US poetry magazines/anthologies. A gay
man, I write psychosociological poetry and describe myself
as a positive thinker. A thread of optimism can be detected
in even the most downbeat of my poems. Poetry publica-
tions include 'August & Genet' (1996) and 'Love and
Human Remains' (2000). My poetry has been placed in
several National Poetry competitions. More details from
RogerTab@aol.com."

FRIENDSHIP

Marriages, they say are made in heaven
But friends, like pearls, are picked and chosen.
Yet blessed are those who possess a friend
Who is steadfast and sincere till the end.
Friends are those who extend a hand
When you are sinking into deep quicksand.

Friends are like candles burning bright
Taking care of you with their guiding light.
Friends are those who are like gluestick,
Through times that are thin and thick,

Friends are those who willingly share
Both mirth and misery with equal care.
Friends are those who lend an ear
To hear your anguish and bring you cheer.

Friends are those who lend their shoulder
In times of distress to make you bolder.
Showers and flowers last for a few hours
But, friendship has power that lasts forever.

Shaffick Hamuth, Forest Gate, London

Mohammed Shaffick Hamuth, author of "Friendship",
said: "I have been writing poems since the age of ten.
Writing verse comes naturally to me. I can write on any
theme and I'm influenced by anything from nature to poli-
tics. I am single and a graduate in economics. I have also
got an excellent academic record and am studying account-
ing and law. I like outdoor recreational activities and I'm
very active in social activities. I also aspire to become a
successful writer one day. Friends, poets or not, can con-
tact me by e-mail at mshamuth@hotmail.com."

THE NIGHT SKY IN JUNE

Yearn for the past,
For bygone days,
For picnics, sea and air.

Yearn for the freedom,
Joy and hope,
Away from every care.

Yearn for the mornings,
Fresh and bright,
Summer evenings bathed in hue.

Yearn for the thoughts,
The dreams, the sport,
The innocence of childhood too.

Yearn for the past,
For days gone by,
As you strive to follow their track.

Yet you know in your heart alas, my friend,
That those days will ne'er come back.

Miriam Bowman, London

Miriam Bowman said: "I enjoy using most mediums. I have
written poems, short stories, essays, articles etc. I have
not yet written a novel. I have had some work published -
two poems, articles and some very short stories. I am
interested in fiction, comedy, drama, love stories, murder
and mystery and thrillers. I particularly enjoy reading clas-
sic literary works, such as Dickens, Shakespeare, Hardy
etc."

IMMIGRANTS PRAYER

Raise your eyes to heaven
Wherever times finds you,
Even though your children sleep
On another continent; and tanks,
Not game boy nintendo stalk
Their dreams.

Raise your hands beyond the
Vapour trails of jets
And know that your sweet wife
Harbours the same hope and
Aspirations you do.
Though you toil in a low paid
Agency and your lodgings leave
A lot to be desired
Know that God works
On your problems
And nothing is too difficult
For him
To achieve.

David Harris, Manor Park, London

David Harris said: "My first poems were about angels and earthworms. I wrote them in an orphanage and they empowered me." For 18 years he travelled as a street musician. "I feel like a homing pigeon always returning to the same themes, unrequited, unconditional love and horticulture addiction. The fabric of my life's woven from these themes, really. I live and work as a gardener in East London, I am married with four children currently making a CD of folk and blues, 'Before and After'." Contact David Harris 226 Grantham Road, London, E12 5ND Tel: 07941 293981.

LETTER TO MUM

Your warmth and tenderness
        are etched on my soul,
You soothe and console me when
        life takes its toll,
Unconditional love is given free no fee
        and I thank you so for loving me.
You're radiant in all you do
        a strength within comes
        shining through,
And when things are tough and life's
        unfair,
You still find love that you can share.
A strong and steadfast heart beats
        deep inside of you,
I wish you so much happiness in everything
        you do.

Gillian Tooth, Hackney, London

TREADING ON...

Here they lay, scattered around my feet
Don't come too near, they are fragile, weak
Just like the spirit, made of the finest porcelain
Invisible to the eye but don't be fooled
I see them,
Speckled brown, matt, empty
There's nothing to lose you know
But you are too frightened to cross my boundary
Less I break too.

Priscilla Westcott, Romford, Essex

STRAIGHT FROM THE HEART

Passion was the fashion.
I wore it on my shirt.
The cause was immaterial
Unlike my tie-dye skirt.

I marched to save the whale.
I marched to save the tree.
I owned a duffel coat-
A badge from CND.

I marched to ban the bomb.
I marched for women's rights.
Passion was the fashion
Like Pretty Polly tights.

Like floppy hats and flares,
Like Andy Warhol art,
Passion was the fashion-
It came straight from the heart.

Yvonne Headington, London

OH MAY IT BE

Oh, may it be a day of lyric sun
Where children romp in rhapsody of fun,
And pussycats purr in drowsy shades of peace,
When mystic bells are tolling my release.
For I have sailed the years of rare champagne,
And no-one treads the broad highway again.
So let the wind be gentle from the west,
And sing of love, and memory ever blest.
I've known the songs of sunshine of the best.
Each friend a true and welcome guest,
With roses and the blossoms of a lane,
The friendly hills, the billows of the main.
The gems of sun have blazed thro' the rain,
And now.... a rapture of a grand refrain.
The poems I have written with grand refrain,
I hope they are not all in vain.
Perhaps I may come on top again.
To lose would be a dreadful shame.
I would have to write them all again,
And then I would have nothing to gain.

Frederich Bathurst, West Ealing, London

WORLD WITHOUT END

And still they watch us.
Alone in our windows,
Their prepubescent eyes follow our every move;
Searching for flaws and imperfections that never were.
We have no sense of direction
In the perpetual Summer of our existence.
Peering below at stairs that lead neither up nor down;
Caught up in the conundrum of not knowing East from
West,
North from South.
Shadows, falling in place of brilliant sunshine,
Shroud the surrounding structures,
Deceiving the mind and defying reason:
Colour is obsolete. Detail is everything.
Imprisoned within our graphite walls like caged animals,
We are observed and studied;
Floating like specimens in a jar.
Him...her...them...us?
The boundaries fade
In a world without end.

Rebecca Kernick, Belsize Park, London

FAT CHOICE

I want to change I don't like what I am...
But I love foods like chocs, cream and ham
I want to be different but know that I can't
Because I take after my mother and aunt!

I know I'm fat and it's not fair
I want to eat everything that's there
It's not true about being fat and happy
Outside I laugh but inside I'm snappy

I want a magic wand to make it happen
To get me out of this awful pattern
I know I've got to help myself
But my motivation gathers dust on a shelf

As I get fatter my esteem gets low
Social invitations are met with a "no"
I hide away so people can't see
This fat person who has become me

I could alter my behaviour and thoughts
Not use words like "shoulds" and "aughts"
I could stay like this forever
Or make a change and be clever!

Shirley Hale, Putney, London

CUPID'S DAGGER

My eyes are cast downward
In a stupefied disbelief.
Where moments ago flowed love,
Is now a deluge of ungoverned grief.

My eyes are filled with unknowing,
My mind is at a loss for laws;
My fingers are useless stitches,
And my palms just hopeless gauze.

What fed the rest of me with life
Will soon utterly be bled.
The once-white shirt she gave me,
Is stained a formless shape of red.

Though my mind has lost its reason,
And floats somewhere above my head,
In its hysterical bewilderment
It replays the single word she said -

A quiet inolongerloveyou
Spoken straight from the heart
Was Cupid's dirty little dagger
That caused this bleeding to start.

Gavin Rodney, Uxbridge, Middlesex

PAIN

Will this pain ever go ...
So you will be back to normal again?
To do all the things you used to do -
Go dancing, go for country walks,
Have friends to dinner,
Cook your favourite dish,
Laughing all around the table -
Happy people
Talking, talking in all directions.
How lovely to have friends
And to do all that you did before,
To be out of pain,
To start life over again!
With God's help, I'm sure this will happen.
He has helped before, so take each day
And don't ask for more.
Each day the pain will be far less,
As it was before.

Ann Sheridan, Hanwell, London

FRIENDSHIP

Friendship is to care and share
Whatever happens to always be there

At times the tide may ebb and flow
Against it all
True friendship grows

Forever friends
Our whole life through
A special bond
Shared with you.

Rosalind Wood, Upminster, Essex

THE GALLEON

The galleon sailed with majestic pride,
Her timbers shivered, but her pain she'd hide.
She creaked and groaned, a mast broke free -
But still she braved the raging sea.

She turned her face into the gale
As ever onward she did sail.
She dipped her bow into the ocean,
Daring the swaying of its motion.

A ship of pride in the dark of night
She fought the waves with all her might.
The sea became calm, like a painted scene -
And she thought of what might have been.

But men care not for pride or rank,
They fired their guns into her flank.
She sank to the bottom, without a moan -
To spend eternity alone!

Mary Baird-Hammond, Chelsea, London

INTENTIONAL BLACKNESS

A small room
Darkness growing from the windows.
The room is full of emptiness
Dogs barking from next door
Chained against a gate.
A distinct smell of urine from corners of the room
A small bed
No pillows
Just an old ripped up sleeping bag.
A little bump
Made by a small boy who sleeps
Dreaming of whiteness
He has never seen the outside.
The door is locked
Or maybe it isn't
The boy was too short to reach the handle.
Trays of moulded porridge
Lying in bowls
Left to rot
Just like the boy.

Rachel Lyon, Forestgate, London

"I write poetry because it is a way of putting my thoughts onto paper where I can always keep them, in case my memory fails me," said **Rachel Lyon.** "My mother and my grandfather played a big role in my determination to keep writing. When I re-read through the poetry I have written I reflect on how I was feeling at the time and the types of things that were running through my mind and over-ran onto the paper. My passion is to share my poetry and observe how the reader interprets it. I would like to thank my grandfather for his honest words and to every one I love dearly. To thank them for painfully having to read through my poetry just to keep me from chasing after them with it."

THE SURVIVOR

Precious pure life joy
Practically snatched from my hands
By someone without
Who entered within
And trespassed forbidden lands
And stripped
The survival yell
Echoed loudly in the empty shell
Barely escaped
To gather strength anew
And reach for the promise
Of love and all its due.

Josephine Idries, London

Josephine Idries said: "I have been writing verse intermittently over a span of 20 years, inspired mainly by events in my own traumatic life history. We all have things that affect us in our lives, sometimes very painful. I just want to share my experiences and perhaps leave a message of hope. I live in London where I run my own personal development workshop, which, like my poetry, looks at discovering and celebrating the greatness, beauty and joy we all have within. If you would like more details about my poetry/workshop send an SAE to Josephine Idries, 14a Norland Square, London, W11 4PX."

THE DARK SIDE

The silence is in my head,
The solitude is agony,
The web keeps on spinning,
It's touching my lips, and the beast is nesting
In my hands...

The fight is always behind my dreams,
The escape is my dream, but my nightmare
Is in my hands...

Jennifer Jeffryes, Enfield, London

Jennifer Jeffryes said: I have been writing poetry since I
was a small child. My inspiration comes from wanting to
share feelings and the emotions we all encounter. I strive to
be able to lighten the sadness of others and hope I can one
day achieve this through my poetry."

RHUBARB!

The acme of success, they say,
Is to have a rose named after you.
Ken Livingstone, ex GLC
And London's new Lord Mayor it's true,
Has gone about things differently.
Not for him the royal majestic way.
He's give his name to a rhubarb.
I kid you not - a rhubarb!

Four years ago, or so they say,
He was approached. Would he bestow
On a stunning new variety
Of rhubarb they'd just begun to grow
His famous name? Ken Laughingly agreed
And so you'll hear today
"Ken Livingstone" is a rhubarb!
You heard me right - a rhubarb!

Politicos have big ideas.
Some work; some don't The free press jeers.
"He talking a load of rhubarb!
A load of old bunkum - rhubarb."

Julia Middleton, Goose Green, London

Julia Middleton said: "I live in South-East London with my husband, Michael who is also a teacher. Apart from writing verse I also write songs and study music at Morley College. My ambition is to write popular songs that sell well. In addition I am a qualified Pentecostal Pastor and have a keen interest in contemporary reworking of traditional ideas of worship, church leadership etc. I am studying Spanish and am interested in the Women's Movements of Liberation Technology in South America. I hope that my religious poetry will be broadcast on World Service and Premier Radio, London's Christian radio station."

PILGRIMAGE

Up the straight and narrow path
Not a flower in sight
So she decked her own way
Bending those golden rules
Of humility and patience
She raced down the pearly lane
Scattering seeds into the stones
Encouraging life and flesh
Bloods and hearts beating
Turning the steep uphill struggle
Into the dallying promenade
Of a pleasure ground thriving
Her knees stopped aching
The path grew fertile
Smoothing into the horizon
Suddenly without realising it
She stood in a primrose filled field.

Michelle Singh, Chelmsford, Essex

Born in Chelmsford **Michelle Singh** enjoys writing, and
reading contemporary literature. "I started writing poetry
and stories when I was five and my work is influenced by
my life experiences, family and university," she explained.
"If anyone asked me to describe my style I would say that I
write with my heart on my sleeve and that I write from
experience." Aged 21 she is a former student with an
ambition to be a published novelist and poet. She recently
graduated from the University of Birmingham with an
English Literature degree. "I have written over a 100
poems and had three poems published and I am currently
writing a novel with help of a creative writing scholarship,"
she added.

THE CORNISH LIZARD

The relentless sea, against the jagged rocks,
So restless the ocean, no vessel could dock.
The cry of the gulls, the wind so fierce,
Natures way, so no man can pierce,
Priviliged I feel so exhilarating this place,
Rocks outstretched arms, to the briney encased.
Carved by time, such caves, ancient within
Maybe the booty of smugglers, brandy and gin
Lifeboat station rejected by years, crumbling and sad,
Seaweed beneath, seen the tides to many to add.
With the neeps and springs, the sailors know,
Out on deck, their home, their only abode.
All that surrounds you, is natures own wonder, no disfig-
ure,
The beauty and splendour, forever leaving a signature.

Jane Ault, Stambourne, Essex

Born in Felixstowe **Jane Ault** enjoys reading, writing, trav-
elling, poetry, gym workouts, shopping, cooking, movies
and visiting places of historical interest. "I started writing
poetry about two years ago," she explained. "I had words
whizzing around in my head and wanted to put them into
verse. My influences are nature and my own experiences
and I would like to be remembered by publishing a book of
poetry and being a happy person." Aged 35 she is former
nurse and now a full-time mother, married to Jeremy, and
they have two small children - Oliver and Cydney-Jane.
She has written several poems but this is the first time she
has had one published. She also aims to write children's
stories. "My biggest fantasy is to be the star of a musical,"
she added.

CHRISTMAS

Everywhere have been signs of Christmas
Trees in windows with twinkling fairy lights
Frosty bells, snowmen stencils on glass panes
Sounds of carol singers in joyful refrains,
People on late shopping hurrying to and fro
Tucked under arms parcels brightly wrapped
calling seasonal greetings to those who they know
santa in his grotto a child upon his knee
Listening earnestly to each one's plea
Mistletoe and holly laughter fills the air
it doesn't matter what's on your christmas table
As long as friends pull up a chair.

R Limage Jones, Grays, Esse

Born in Sutton Veni in Wiltshire **Rose Ann Jones** enjoys
art, crafts, writing song lyrics and bowling. "I started writing poetry when my first child was born in 1964," she said.
"I sent a poem to my mother to tell her how I felt. My work
is influenced by personal events and I would describe my
style as eventful and heartfelt. I would like to be remembered for my poetry and music lyrics." Aged 59 she is a
library assistant with an ambition to win a bowling competition so that she can write about her victory. She is widowed with two children and the person she would most like
to be for a day is a singer. She has written many poems
and had several published. She has also written children's
stories. "The persons I would most like to meet are Bruce
Forsyth and Matthew Kelly because I see them as persons I
would like to be," she added.

THE JOYS OF PARENTHOOD

Have you a daughter of age 16 plus?
Who can fill you with pride or an urge to cuss.
Does she give the impression she's older than you?
That your worldly wisdom is barely worth a sou.
Your knowledge of present day culture is pretty dismal
And your understanding of modern youth rather abysmal.
Your experiences of your early days are archaic
And your reflections on contemporary life boring and
prosaic.
If you have - join the universal parental club,
There's no escaping the encounter, there's the rub.
You'll fare no better 'til she has a child of her own
When at last you may see the fruit of the seeds you have
sown.
She'll then have some understanding of your current
frustration
When she runs foul of the same attitudes that create your
parental agitation.

Allen Jessop, Merton Park, London

SITTING HERE

Sitting here, all I can do is think,
Nothing much else to do.
Life passes me by,
Speeding past in a perpectuous blur,
Stillness sucks me in,
Unmoving, resting, dying,
What life I lead is no longer here,
The absence apparent in the oppressing silence,
All civilisation is lost,
In this monotonous undertone that is life.
Who is responsible for all this normality?
Sitting here, all I can do is think
There is nothing else to do.

Amy Hagan, Canvey Island, Essex

TOGETHER

I take you by the hand as we stride together up the hill,
The breeze gently sighing, telling us how we feel,
remembering the day the boy took the girl and felt her,
and set her upon that one great helter skelter.

The people on the ground below
screamed and, oh god, how they cried
whilst the girl did was shake and shriek down the slide
where he caught her, held her and loved her until the day
they died.

I take you by the hand as we walk together, stride by
stride,
ever upwards, past the thunder and rain
past the hurt and past the pain till we stop,
smile and run free! and there we will remain!

Emma Knuckey, Southend on Sea, Essex

WITH EYES CLOSED

Around me there are no more wars.
My neighbours voices rise to praise one another
They do not lift their fists to fight.

There are marching bands along the streets
I hear their feet, anxious.
There are sirens of celebration.

My fingers touch two different markings
Enemies
Lying side by side in blissful sleep.

Pounding behind me, now pass me
Children at play perhaps.
Bang! Bang!

Firecrackers? Perhaps.
And the world is a much better place
When I observe with eyes closed.

Urslin Constantine, Barking, Essex

PRING 2000

An early Spring, how good to see
The blossom on the cherry tree,
The crocuses with colours bright,
The daffodils a blaze of light.
The time of year for all creation
To start another generation.

But all across the clear blue sky
Streak trails from aircraft low and high
As though some careless child had scrawled
In chalk across a clear blue board.
Where could all this pollution go
But fall upon the earth below?

On sprouting shoots all green and new,
On daffodil and crocus too,
On nesting birds and bumble bees,
On cherry blossom in the trees
Upon that welcome springtime scene
All too briefly new and clean.

Stella Elliott, Romford, Essex

THAT PLEASANT FACE

That pleasant face
Always wears a smile
As in life's race
We approach the final mile

First a T.I.A
Followed by a stroke
So day by day
Her life it is no joke

Yet even now
She laughs at her mistakes
But knows not how
Her brain, wrong turning takes

We laugh together
I hope we always will
But wonder whether
Can we climb this hill

While we remain
As always, man and wife
I could not gain
A better companion for life.

John Sharp, Burnham on Crouch, Essex

THE FIRST DAY OF SPRING

I wandered through the countryside
On the very first day of Spring,
And the beauty and tranquillity
Made my heart, with the birds, want to sing.
Buds were bursting into leafy green,
Pussy willow and catkins could be seen.
A squirrel scampered across my path
And nearby sparrows enjoyed a mud bath.
Rabbits frolicked in the sun until they saw they
were watched by someone.
Little lambs skipped about in the field,
Whilst overhead noisy seagulls wheeled.
Daffodils held their golden heads high,
Larks soared and tumbled in the sky.
Across the meadow church bells rang out,
Calling to evensong the devout.
The sun began to sink in the west,
And birds flew homeward to find their nest.
On such a perfect day as this,
To be alive is surely, bliss.

Audrey Wright, Romford, Essex

THE STING

I'm not a cash dispenser Paul,
In fact, I have no cash at all.
You think my purse is a bottomless pit
And I can keep giving you cash from it
But you know that money doesn't grow on trees
It's earned by busy little bees
Called Mum and Dad
Working hell for leather
To keep this little hive together
And your contributions way overdue
Now I want some cash from you.
So listen up, here's how it goes
This cashpoint sign is reading CLOSED!

B Mooney, Canvey Island, Essex

NATURE'S RHYTHM

Slow beats the primal heart of ebb and tide,
Of rise and fall, encroachment and retreat.
The narrow runnels grow to rivers wide
To shrink again at ebb, a ceaseless beat.

And yet, for all it's changes, there is constancy.
A rhythm, fixed, as day must follow night,
As sun will follow moon in silent potency
Returns the world, unerring, to the light.

The seasons have their place, the warmth returns.
The boy grows into man, from seed the tree.
The storms will pass, the glorious sunshine burns.
Each time we meet there is just you and me...

Robert Hallmann, Benfleet, Essex

STAGE FRIGHT

Knees knocking, fingers twitching,
Eyes popping, nose running ...
Standing paralysed, before two
Hundred heads, waiting amongst
darkness, for some gesture or
reaction.

Nothing, no sound,
Just despair, over powering sense
Of annihilation.
Hissing, booing, disappointment.
The eager anticipation wearing
thin and dispelling.

A nightmare from hell,
Rooted to the spot,
Nothing to sell.
An audience not interested,
Not intent now,
Slowly, Bodies leaving from
Seats.

Emotions, swirling in turmoil,
Rushing round the soul.
Fierce force of gusto,
Performer leaves stage right.

Lee Dohoo, Shoeburyness, Essex

FREEDOM

Take my spirit to the skies little bird
So I may see all around and not be heard
Let the freedom of your wings carry me
From the body, no more pain, set me free

Let my spirit roam the world all the year
And let my loved ones know there's no more fear
For I'll be with them in my mind can't they see
That it was their love that finally set me free.

Jane Sagrott, Benfleet, Essex

GRIM REAPER

Grim Reaper, you're a scumbag,
I'm not afraid of you,
You're nothing to be scared of,
You're a slave of destiny too.

You go where you are told to go,
By a power bigger than yours,
The deity who rules us all
Sends you to far off shores.

And tells you just whose time is up,
And just who to collect,
Decisions do not fall to you,
So much to your regret.

You're just as much a slave as me,
You do as you are told,
You have no say in who goes when,
Or whom you must enfold.

Mick Nash, Corringham, Essex

THROUGH THE EYES OF AN ANGEL

Floating through a tunnel
Enveloped by a blackness
As I move on forwards the veil of darkness lifts
And I am bathed in radiant light
Appearing before me like a silhouette through swirling
mists.

With a halo of gold and a robe snow white
A celestial angel unfolding her wings
Cradles me with much tenderness
In surrounding love and warmth
As a baby in its mother's womb
So I am bonded to her with fine silver cord
Through the eyes of an angel
I can be no master of disguise
The very depths of soul stripped bare can hold no secrets.

For the persona to be scruntinized
No longer one of a crowd for I have been
Cleansed and purified from the inside out
This heavenly paradise that stands at my feet
With pathways carpeted a golden luminous glow
Has given me inner peace and made my life complete.

Helen Gust, Penge, London

*To my family and best friend who have given me
tremendous encouragement and fulfilled my life in many
special ways.*

A TRUE FRIEND

Special people were made to see us through
The good times and the bad times too,
A person on whom we can depend,
Someone we can call a friend!

A true friend is always there for you
As often as can be!
They comfort you when you feel down,
Although you disagree!

But the real test comes when the bad times arrive
When you're in the worst times of strife.
A real friend will stay and help you through,
And will be around for the rest of your life!

Stacey Wager, Chelmsford, Essex

"I wrote my first poem at the age of seven because I wanted
to write down my feelings," said **Stacey Wager** who enjoys
swimming, writing and tennis. Age 16 she was born in
Chelmsford. She is still at school and has an ambition to
become a journalist. "My poetry is influenced by friends,
family, personal feelings and situations," she said. "My
style is casual, playful but honest and I would like to be
remembered for my fun-loving attitude to life and my
cheerful personality. "The person I would most like to be
for the day is my mother and I have always looked up to
Jill Dando because her work inspired me to be a journal-
ist." Stacey has written short stories, newspaper articles
and many poems but this is the first poem she has had
published.

AT PEACE

Natural or a gift
Faces, places and tasties
To serve with a nerve
Or Beethoven that is forever.

To be practical was there
many a war, they say look
offer the poor, though some
survive better than others
there's always a time for lovers.

Don't gossip too much or play
to call a card the national guard
for when we see we agree
When we listen the trees will glisten.

To be born with a brain to train
will it rain for the world to stay sane
And when there is women
Perhaps now not a dual.

Susan White, Canvey Island, Essex

Born and brought up on Canvey Island, **Susan White** is a
bookshop owner who has already had 11 of her poems
published. She said: "I have written a book 'History of
Canvey Island, Five Generations', which is available from
243 Eastern Esplanade, Canvey Island, Essex at £9.99. I
started writing during my teens, my other hobbies are
reading, swimming, history and learning Spanish as my
parents own a villa in Almeria, Spain. I was educated at
Timberlog School in Basildon, Grays Technical College and
Charlotte Mason Teachers Training College and taught PT
in schools in Luton and Stanford-le-Hope."

IT'S NOT A CRIME

The saying goes, life is too short
Without a smile, never to be caught.
A person to give a word of kind
A hug, and kiss, and you will find
Your days are better, may seem longer,
When folk are blue, you make them stronger.
As showing your love, sharing their tears you help dispel
their nasty fears.
As people pass, a smile to them give
As through this life you learn to live
each full moment, a day at a time,
Smile and be happy, it's not a crime.

Elaine Mumford, Leigh on Sea, Essex

Born in London **Elaine Mumford** enjoys crosswords and
sport for the disabled. "I started writing poetry from a
young age just for enjoyment," she explained. "My work is
influenced by Patience Strong and my style is sentimental.
I would like to be remembered for my caring ability, listen-
ing ear, my shoulder to cry on and my wicked sense of
humour." Aged 55 she is a former registered nurse, now
disabled and has ambitions to excel in sports for the dis-
abled, be a good wife, cheer people, live a happy life, and to
fly in a plane or helicopter. She is married to Steven and
they have two children. "The person I would most like to
meet is Jimmy Saville because I admire all his work," she
said. Although she has written many poems this was the
first poem she submitted for publication. She has also
written short stories.

UNTITLED

February brings the rain, that's what the poets say
and the long dark days of Winter filled me with dismay.
But as I walked around my garden I saw a wondrous sight.
The dark green spears of daffodils were reaching to the
light.
I walked a little further and there, beneath the trees,
a drift of pure white snowdrops were trembling in the
breeze.
A bowl of purple pansies, viburnum pink and sweet,
the spotted leaves of lungwort there beneath my feet
Catkins on the hazel tree waving at the sky,
while a clump of yellow primula nod their heads nearby.
And somewhere up above my head a bird began to sing
and suddenly I realised that was nearly Spring.
The long, dark days of Winter would quickly fade away
and the longed for Summer sunshine would soon be on its
way.

Jacqueline Harnett, Hockley, Essex

TODAY'S THE DAY!

Today's the day we hide our tears,
Chat idly to conceal our fears,
Churning inside the butterflies
Hidden obscured from searching eyes
And muffle pulse in topmost gear.

Appear relaxed, veiled fine veneer
Behind our guard each disappear,
Coupled steadfast, braced strong allies
As today's the day!

Await the hour in strange new sphere
Zenith moment or grim nadir?
Pray the outcome will gratify
With loss of reins life runs awry
Grappling to hold or see course clear,
Because today's the day!

Hilary Robson, Westcliff on Sea, Essex

FLOWERS

Flowers are red,
Flowers are blue,
Flowers are all around,
But are they true.

Flowers are tall,
Flowers are short,
Flowers in shops,
And a poppy I have bought.

Flowers grow in the ground,
Flowers grow in pots,
They fill the garden with colour,
And I like them lots and lots.

Flowers grow in winter,
Flowers grow in spring,
Flowers grow under wind chimes,
That make a wonderful ding.

Natasha Bentley, Rochford, Essex

MASSAGE

As I travel across the seas to hold my mind with yours
To entangle my body with yours engaging as one
Your odour permeates my senses, all I taste is you
A light headiness overcomes me, as I'm thinking of you
Euphoric as one we rise on the tide
You in my head, you all around
I feel your heat from within
Our souls unite, fused together
We carry ourselves as one to eternity.

Barbara Davies, Southend on Sea, Essex

THINK GREEN

It lays in big pits and that's where it sits
Until those big diggers arrive
We're told it will rot, are we sure, I think not
All we do is put toxic gas in the sky

It's done as a trend, but to us it depends
On what will happen later
But what I can see, gas escapes free
And destroys the ozone with a crater

It's time to be smart, so why don't we start
By discarding our waste more wisely
The reason for this I have to insist
Or this will all turn into blighty

So don't be in haste by dumping your waste
It all can be put to good use
Paper and board, we can all afford
And we're all to blame for the abuse.

Andy Tremayne, Wickford, Essex

PARLEZ VOUS FOOTBALL

Footballers in bygone days,
Were Smith and Jones, and Brown.
They played for their own country,
Or they played for their home town.

If they should get a transfer,
They joined a similar pack.
A Smith and Jones were forward,
And a Brown was at the back.

But now if you go to football,
And as you sit on a bench
You should have a phrase book with you,
In Italian, German or French.

In each team a Brazilian,
Or an African or two,
But if you're Smith or Jones or Brown,
There's no team place for you.

Len Spooner, South Woodham Ferrers, Essex

MUSIC

Music is a food
It nourishes the soul
It needs no preparation
It creeps in any hole.

The poorest can make it
With no cost to anyone
A bit of wood, a shell,
Can give tremendous fun.

It needs no other language
To form a common bond
An excellent therapy
With no medicinal wand

It plays a part in any life,
whether damaged or whole
Make sure you welcome music
Into your stress filled bowl.

Janice Thornton, Leigh on Sea, Essex

GREENER PASTURES

You can't take me
my hands are tied
you won't redeem
the beauty has died

Do you see me crying
over everything spilt
has the formality been met
over childish guilt

You took me over
you think you know
I've left your face
for me to grow

A miracle in place
you're not so young
confusion state
my locks undone

In the eye I've met the maker
we are the given path
the fate of introverted wisdom
takes breath in the aftermath.

Michelle Hurley, Elm Park, Essex

BRING FORTH YOUR FRESH GREEN SHOOTS

Bring forth your fresh green shoots,
Bring forth your smouldering sun,
Bring forth your starlite nights,
When you day is almost done.

The dawn has come upon us,
It spreads across the land.
It brings with it the sunbeams,
As we gently stroll, hand in hand.

Hand in hand, with nature
In one, with all around
The gentle song of life,
Come's whispering from the ground.

We pass this way but once,
So be gentle with this place,
Because, the things we do today.
In the future our children, must face.

Brian Marett, Southend on Sea, Essex

A GEORDIE LASS

A Geordie lass,
She pinched my ass,
She pinched it right here.

A Geordie lass
She pinched my ass,
She went in with no fear.

She didn't go in gentle,
She got a nice firm grip,
I tried to pinch her credentials,
But she gave me the slip.

It happened in Newcastle
On the stairs at WH Smiths,
I wish it had been Woolworths
Cos they had working lifts.

A Geordie lass
She pinched my bum,
Some may say that's cheeky.

A Geordie lass,
She pinched my ass,
So now I go to Newcastle weekly.

David Woodcock, Southend on Sea, Essex

CAN WE CELEBRATE THESE DAYS?

I saw this old boy in the church doorway,
but his only faith was in a bottle of booze.
And as for the ex choirboys, well their god is shot with the
drugs they use.
What about the girl on the street corner?
Her angel vanished in the wishing well,
Doesn't matter that she's a sinner she's living out her hell.
Can religion can find them now? as their bright lives fade
to grey.
Is there a heaven in the clouds or did they scare that God
away?
Although they may hate this world and its phoney sins
They won't ask God to let them in
Old man's faith in a bottle of gin.
The boys have got a needle with their angles in.
As children this future was bright
We could sow our wildest dreams across society's field .
But now the reality glows like the night
And religion is no longer one's faith but man's shield.

Lucy Hunt, Burnham on Crouch, Essex

MUM KNEW BEST

I wish I had listened to what my mother said,
Pay attention to your teachers let their knowledge fill your
head.

The best years of your life are when you are at school,
Don't waste time being stupid, playing around, acting the
fool.

Attend school every single day and never turn up late,
Or mess around with local boys outside the school main
gate.

Hand in your homework every day and work on it at night,
And if at first you don't succeed persevere to get it right.

If only I had listened and let the penny drop,
I'd be earning a far better wage than working in a shop!

Jan Wickens, Aveley, Essex

SOMERFIELD REVERIE

On Monday I went food shopping,
For just ordinary stuff, it was an ordinary day,
Margarine, flour, bread, milk and bananas,
It was cold out and the sky was grey.

Standing there in Somerfield, I began sorting out what
they'd got,
Wrapped bananas large and expensive, and ones that were
small and not,
I noticed on the labels, they came from many a place,
Columbia, Venezuela, The Windward Islands,
"The Windward Islands!"

I felt the sun kiss my face!
Saw it burning out of a sky into a sea of azure blue,
Heard fronds of palm trees rustle, as parrots darted
through ,
Monkeys chattered and played on the beach and Jasmine
scented the air,

I was buying bananas, in Somerfield!!
But for that moment, felt I really was there,
Just that place name on a label, and my mind
transported me away,
What began as an ordinary Monday, became an extraordi-
nary day!

Marion Durrant, Ockendon, Essex

GOD'S CREATURES

All God's creatures large and small
Short and tall he loves
Them all
They all have the right
To be
Happy like you and me
Love is everywhere we all
Play a part
"You have lots to share
Look into your heart
People everywhere sometimes
Feel their pain
Whether they are black or white
Let us all be friends.

Zoe Doyle, Hornchurch, Essex

SANITY

What fool would rise at crack of dawn?
Leave a bed and woman soft and warm!
I am that fool, the reason why.
To flirt once more with sanity.
To see Lake Bassenthwaite, vast and still
Sunshine rising o'er yonder hill.
To listen to bird song, near and far.
Without intrusion of man and car.
To restore ones faith in our mankind
Realise, there are wondrous views to find.
To recharge the batteries of fragile man.
To see a little of gods gifts and plan to flirt with sanity, in
this mad world. Peace, contentment, like a flag unfurled.

Leonard Wildman, Rayleigh, Essex

A MOMENT

We were alone just the two of us.
A moment in time that will always be captured,
with my granddaughter and I.
I touched her face and she touched mine.
We had stared at each other for the very first time
She of about six months with no understanding
but I became aware that we both had
something new and we we exploring each other very
silently.
Everything else was so still and quite with such warmth
I drew her close and the tears welled up in my eyes
That moment I recognised my baby granddaughter
as another human being
Both of us needing love
This special love of a human touch and
understanding of each other all the days of our lives.

Sylvie Sorrell, Dagenham, Essex

SOUL SURVIVING

Her tender bones need healing, her pretty face needs repair
Fun she was intending, but its ended in despair
Her golden hairs the colour of the blood within her veins
Life is hanging by a thread, do we know who holds the
reins
Within, her heart is pounding, a firm and steady beat
The damage to her body, is a challenge it will meet
Her eyes take in surroundings and lightness seems to loom
Her minds turned off the button, to scared to face the
doom
The doctors job is over, the broken bones are set
But the healing of the soul within, isn't over yet
The heart starts pounding faster and the brain turns on
the light
Together in their battle for her life, they must fight
As night turns into daytime and sun rises overhead
Her spirit finally comes to life and we know the soul's not
dead.

Sandi Evans, Basildon, Essex

THE FEELING OF LOVE

I love you so much it's almost untrue,
I can't imagine my life without you,

Words cannot describe my feelings of love,
Sometimes it's hard to believe you're not sent from above,

The way you look at me makes my heart melt,
This is the most love I have ever felt,

I love the feeling I get from looking in your eyes,
It sends me floating up to the skies,

I wish I could tell you the way I feel,
But this secret I will leave for you to unreel.

Hollie Salter, Brentwood, Essex

OM SHANTI

When the mind is truly focused
And the thoughts contained therein,
The intellect will sift the chaff
And blow it to the wind
When emotion clouds all reasoning
And it's hard to broach the storm
Just give in to a mighty force
That's born of inward calm.
Let the peace you feel take over
Quieten discord, feel content
Never letting troubles bother you
Never letting anger vent.
For to find that certain countenance
Should be every persons goal
To meet each moment with the hope
Of a quiet and peaceful soul.

Yvonne Sparkes, Chelmsford, Essex

SPRINGTIME

Spring is here, birds start to sing,
The grass is greener, the bulbs start to bring
Lovely colour to cheer us, after wintertime,
Children playing outside, washing out on the line
The sun is bright, after dull dreary days
Just the medicine we need in so many ways.
After being shut in with dark early nights
Go for a walk, see the beautiful sights,
Of the country in bloom. now that spring is here,
The blossom on trees, we have longed for all year,
Who needs luxuries when all that is free.
As it was given to you and me.
So enjoy the springtime and lovely fresh air
Sing like the birds, let down your hair,
Everything comes alive, when the sun shone
Let's all enjoy it before it has gone,
Daffodils swaying in a line
Tells us all it is Springtime.

Peggy Wheeler, Basildon, Essex

*I dedicate my poem to my late darling husband Bob, for 50
happy years together, who inspired me to write.*

LUPUS

Lupine lope
soft as snow.
Grey on white on brown
ghost glimpse through trees.
Siren yellow eyes devour the horizon
and inward laughs a hungry grin,
or,
in sombre moon mood,
sings.
Bunched muscle,
Bristle fur,
A flash of violence:
Wolf

Susan Sparkes, Woodford Green, Essex

JUST NUMBERS

Age is just a state of mind,
And it's best to be philosophical I find.
Some people fear the big 5 0,
But it's only a number, don't they know?
Some days you think you're 25,
And feel like you could jump and jive.
At other times you feel like 88,
And think you'll soon be at the pearly gates.
Take life a day at a time,
Who cares if you're no longer 29.
Accept your age whatever it may be,
Whether it's 35, 60 or 43.
It's a waste of time wishing you were still 21,
It's no good looking back, the past is done.
When asked your age, tell it with pride,
People just laugh when they know you've lied.

Peggy Stoker, Canvey Island, Essex

BUBBLES

Soft, shimmering,
The glass mirage of a thousand tiny
Bubbles float aimlessly around my mind,
Each a quota off happiness,
A measure of bliss.
Transient, beautiful,
The immortal effervescence
Captured forever as one
Lights, with cold, butterfly wings,
Upon my palm.
Shimmering helplessly
This rainbow of opportunities
Trembles, as I hold it, not daring to breathe.
An eternity passes,
Waiting for the final blow,
Watching the glass shatter in my mind.
All the time, watching, waiting,
Watching fragile destiny,
Cowering and cold in my palm,
Awaiting the end.

Sarah Bidgood, Danbury, Essex

DARKNESS

As darkness casts a shadow
Upon your crystal skin
The prism of light
Transmission ends.

Stars glisten through the ether
Waiting for my eyes to deliver
There is a universal sight to see
Sitting underneath this tree.

As the aura of the night
Seems to come from within
The colours shimmer and ignite the sky.

The darkness was engulfed by light
As the aura faded out of sight
Watching you watching me
Hoping that this dream will be.

David Brookes, Romford, Essex

A HIDDEN WORLD TO ENCOUNTER

The past, the future, the present,
Thinking, remembering, forgetting,
One's truth about the past may fade,
though deeply hidden inside the soul,
lies the memories of one, lightened or black as a hole.

Certainties of a treasured or horror moment,
Something hypnotising one's mind to stop, think look or
approach.
Being the best way, it may grow into a smear,
Or one's own experience, worth remembering. may feel for-
gotten causing a fear.

The existence is always with you,
Your picture, your memory,
intruders cannot enter, to take what is so precious,
only you see it.
Letting go of the past may enhance to terrify,
Never does it leave, unless you try to let it die.

Persevere with the needs in your life,
may your dreams go on, and not be shattered,
In a sense of doing or remembering,
it is continuously on doing,
the past the future the present.

Corinna Collins, Grays, Essex

OLD AGE TOGETHER

What though your face is wrinkled,
What though your hair is grey,
To me you're still the lovely girl
I married yesterday.

What though your breasts are sagging,
What do I care for that!
What though your once firm tummy,
Has turned to rolls of fat.

What though your legs are grossly veined,
Your once trim ankles thick,
What though you walk so slowly,
You have to use a stick.

Your eyes are soft and gentle,
Your smile has lots to say,
For I still love you dearly,
My girl of yesterday.

Cynthia Berry, Frinton on Sea, Essex

24 HOURS

It twists and turns and changes with age,
Loving, need, heartache and dependency.
Each day different than the last,
Although with the same similarities of the moon rising and
the sun setting.
So many changes,
So many mistakes,
So many regrets,
So many questions needing answers.
Fearing that precious moments will end and all that will be
left are memories,
That we will leave this life without making a difference.
Fearing that the world is just a dream and someday the
dreamer will wake, and then what?

Gemma Marie Crane, Canvey Island, Essex

WHAT IS LOVE?

What is love?
That tingly feeling when he is near
The pounding of your heart
That skips a beat with both excitement and fear.

That first gentle kiss
That sets your soul free
High up into the clouds
Seems never ending.

But soon the romance is over
And you are left once again
sad, alone and unwanted
Tormented by memories you once had.

Laura Rydings, Grays, Essex

MY MIND'S EYE

Around me I see the world passing by.
Why can't the evil fly away?
The rain is beating down upon my roof.
Why can't the sunshine stay?
The eyes inside my head are crying
And the people outside my door are dying.

I'm surrounded by the ugly truth.
You wouldn't expect that from a youth.
Nobody understand or listens to me.
I just can't make them see
That we are killing ourselves with fear.
And some say this is a special year.

I am faced with Hell everywhere I go
Because of the terrible things I know.
Money and death are in charge here
And I cannot help but shed a tear.
But inside my mind I can find
The joy of my mind's eye.

Andrew Humphrey, South Woodham Ferrers, Essex

MEMORIES

A village in the heart of Kent
to the primary school I went
my house was built
just like the church it stands alone.

On the corner the village inn
hoppickers have gathered they drink and sing
they arrive on the old steam train
pick the hops and go again.

Across the road the blacksmith
with shire horses stand
with their brasses gleaming in the sun
they look so very grand.

Up the little hill you climb
the village hall in sight
made of wood and painted green
there's a dance on Friday night.

The fish and chip man comes once a week
for the village family treat
to the playing field where I used to play
me memories are here to stay.

Mary Simpson, Wickford, Essex

Mary Simpson is a 56-year-old housewife who has an ambition to continue to live a long and happy life. She is married to John and they have one child. Mary was born in Kent and her hobbies include gardening and dog showing. "I started writing poetry several years ago for recreation," she remarked. "My work is influenced by things around me and my style is rustic. I would like to be remembered for my lifestyle." She has written over 20 poems and had four published. "The person I would most like to meet is David Bellamy because of his love for country life," she said. "My worst nightmare is to have the green belt area where I live taken away for building."

AS ANGELS DESCEND

Darkness falls upon this day
It's shadows fall upon my face
Masking eyes that ache with hope
That tomorrow will come
With the glow of angels
With their hands to soothe
This aching head
With blinding light to consume
These shadows
With their silken voices
To calm these fears
And as they descend upon
This day
They light the way into tomorrow
Their eyes luminous
Beckoning me,
Calling me
Back into life.

Carrie Stonebridge, Canvey Island, Essex

MADNESS IS MY SANITY

The voices which scream at me from within my head,
Are also my friends who I sleep with in bed.
And when I rock back and forth and then from side to side
I sometimes feel as if I am free and sailing on high tide.
Throwing myself against this padded cell wall,
I secretly smile and think to myself that really you are the fool.
For all you do is drug me and then closely observe
My strange and unpredictable behaviour which plays havoc with your nerves.
You may well think that I am mad, but then equally so are you,
Because you can cry tears of happiness, yet also when you are blue.
Don't even bother trying to understand the workings of my mind,
It's really no different to yours, so what do you expect to find?
And give up trying to cure me, as my craziness keeps me sane.
Instead why not consider society, as aren't they always the ones to blame.

Elizabeth Smith, Saffron Walden, Essex

GALACTIC ELDERS

From outer space deep outer space,
The pulsating engines hum and race,
Who's coming now to planet Earth,
From the darkness of the universe.

Men of Earth are watched and seen,
People and places on their screen,
Mankind still in his infancy,
With opening eyes that cannot see.

The watchers are looking very intent,
The dying of the innocent,
The senseless wars still going on,
Slaughter and grief all day long.

The lessons that are still not learned,
Signs and messages completely spurned
The silent watchers look concerned
Nothing it seems is being turned.

The time is not right for us to be,
With opening eyes that cannot see,
mortal man he may wait too long,
I hear the engines humming on.

Jim Wilson, Westcliff on Sea, Essex

SEA'S EDGE

Into the spume-washed air, the ridge
Of diamond-glinted rock breaks through.
Sunlit above, cold-shadowed where
The secret current swirls beneath.

There, where grey pebbles silent clash
Sand in mosaic patterns drifts.
A mirror-image of the clouds
Wind-urged above, curling and tossed,
Ready to plunge, re-form and fade,
Vanish like smudged and silvery smoke.

The shore line, fringed with glistening weed,
Battered by raging, wrenching tides
Remains a battlefield between
Fury and animosity.
The violent anger of the waves
And the defiant, shifting stones.

Nancy Johnson, Clacton on Sea, Essex

METAMORPHOSIS

Memories of a past so beautiful to me,
Dissolutions in a child that is all I can see
Trapped in a mind filled with beauty and peace
So secure in that dream is where I long to be
But reality called my name some day back then
Subjected me to a world filled with darkness and gloom
Sorrow and pain is the name that came
Faithless and selfish is what I became
Memories of a child is where I will begin.
To start my life all over again
With God being the stem one day at a time
Through guidance I will grow to leave
faithlessness and selfishness behind
From my stem springs a flower blooming
beautifully in the sun
With care and guidance spiritually at one is where I'll be
Now my thoughts are filled with how fragile we be
And how life last no longer than a dream
So to prepare myself for what will be is all that is left for
me.

Sonia Bowen, Aveley, Essex

STEPS

Wherever we have been happy, those bright places
Live within us, vibrant and unchanged,
Are drawn together in the inner landscape,
Nothing omitted, nothing rearranged.

An oil lamp's pungent smell and yellow flicker
Open the sense doors to that timeless place.
I am returned to Grandfather's humble kitchen
And the smile of welcome on his wizened face.

But time is incoherent, we cannot fathom
The straight path forward, till we realise
Only those footsteps that have moved the spirit
Are real steps in the personal paradise.

Pamela Constantine, Upminister, Essex

MY HEART'S GUILTY CONSCIENCE

Have you ever wondered where your conscience lies
It lies in your heart with many do or dies
As a result of your lies your heart beats in shame
It sends a cry of help through your veins
And as these secrets and lies build up through the years
Your heart will, shed a solemn tear
Just as your heart learns to live with your fears
You'll find it beats slower till it stops in its tracks
But have you ever wondered what drove it to that?
Don't bottle up your feelings you don't have to be pure
Don't shut people out
Or your guilty conscience will kill you for sure.

Emma Keenan, South Woodham Ferrers, Essex

DAZED NIGHTS

Another world exists above and far beyond my window.
It watches my every move.
Dancing a slow lingo, nothing to prove.

I sit and gaze,
cigarette smoke lingers in the air,
engulfing the lapse of time.

Some nights it vanishes out of sight, banished.
With all my might I close my eyes and I can see,
God Himself
From His eyes
It pains me to see His sorrow.

My hand trembles with fear as I wave goodbye.
I feel myself falling to the ground
The pain lifts from my soul.

As I hurtle to my death
I realise what a mistake it was
and that I wish I had been found.

Now I am the one out of sight.
I watch myself from another world
contemplating my death.

Michelle Read, Manningtree, Essex

MYTH

Can a heart break?
Tough vital organ
Beating out
Life's rhythmic tune
From womb to tomb.
Can a heart break?
Soul singers say it will
But this I know
Although they tell us so
It cannot break
But oh! how it can ache.

Marion P Webb, Bromley, Kent

LOVE AT FIRST SIGHT

The world is so peaceful,
The sky is blue;
The sun shines brightly
For me and you.
Our eyes meet,
Our arms entwine;
Love is so strong
That life just seems fine.
No need to speak
Our eyes tell so much,
A hint of a kiss
The tenderest touch.
Fire ignites
Through heaven we fly;
Life is such fun
With you nearby.

Verity Burgess, Chelmsford, Essex

LOVE?

What is love? How can we know?
A word, a gesture, that secret look.
Are they signs of this emotion?
For on we go, causing this pain.
Yet then we say 'I love you' again and again.

Surely 'love' doesn't encompass what you give,
Taunting, spite, anger so often bestowed.
The countless times of tears which flow,
Then 'sorry' is said, flowers are sent
And all is well, forgiven once again.

Around and around we go, no progress is made,
Our love seems so deep, yes, we do care,
But take a step back, and analyse,
It is dying, wilting so rapidly,
Watch it deteriorate, not intensify.

On we go, fooling ourselves we're fine,
While its clear if we do carry on
We'll only despise each other for lying,
The light has died, remember how it shone?
Let's leave it now and be the friends we once were.

Raffalina Peluso, Westcliff on Sea, Essex

MISSING YOU

It's been a long time,
Although you're still the same,
From far away I see you,
Strolling by.

The heart beats quicken,
A passing thought,
A memory as some say.

Strangers we seem,
Numbness enters,
For a moment,
Then quickly goes away.

Another time,
Another day.

Nina McLeod, Southend on Sea, Essex

THE SPRING

You hear the sound
Before you see it.
In the midst of the ordinary garden,
Water suddenly issues from stone
Polishing permanently the tarmac of the drive.
One of the four elements,
The stuff of life,
Like a holy well
At your door,
Entering with your wet footsteps.

Mary O'Keeffe, Ashford, Kent

LIMITS

in liquid prison
where passion is punished
or lies hostage on the block

so much smoke
and vegetal rot
from the dung heap

light showers have started
light hovers at the window
light lights up the liquid

blue smokes the clouds
blood drips to the floor
this shoddy mosaic
year after year

as fungus grows
around the floor
and liquid melts
mid air

Jean Owen, Westcliff on Sea, Essex

A HEART UP YOUR SLEEVE (ACE GIRL)

With the passing of a wintry spell,
Into your arms my poor heart fell,
Beating to a tender strain
That o'er my soul shall ever reign.
The velvet words of your creation
Will always be my inspiration,
Bewitching me with mighty charms,
My heart you haul into your arms.

My total flame I hereby give,
That you in sunny scope may live,
So cast away your heavy woe,
And let your godlike merit grow.

Your elegance awakens me,
Imparting all the light I see,
That from you handsome smile doth beam
To turn my day into a dream.
The bed to which I will retire
Is warm with love and will inspire
The honest thought that I here draft
That you are here by Heaven's craft.

Stephen Moles, Chelmsford, Essex

FOLLY IN FLANDERS

Mutely they stand, these weathered stones,
in place of flesh and blood and bones,
from yesteryear the Smiths and Jones.
Forgotten now, save in the lives
of ageing friends and widowed wives.
Gone with the glory once displayed
by men of State, who undismayed,
caused flowering youth to fall and fade.

In Flanders Field beneath the plough
the war torn earth has settled now,
except the ploughman brings to light
a riven skull whose baleful stare
will question yet again the right
to sacrifice the many there.

No wreaths, or flags, or poppies red
can justify the wasted dead.

Ron Dean, Saffron Walden, Essex

STRAIGHT FROM THE HEART

Our hearts unite, they do not coerce
Like the rhythm and rhyme of a poetic verse
A natural flow, from me to you
Straight from the heart, pure and true.

Like a gentle stream, sparkling with delight
Effervescent, in the sunlight bright.
Shimmering ripples, dance and play
For our hearts, are bright and gay.

Like wisps of fragrance, in the air
Our love cascades, for all to share
Our beauty our pleasure, becomes surreal
With the joy, of love, that we both feel.

With the morning birdsong, the dew on the grass
a brand new day, our love to a mass
Of special moments spent with you
The love in my heart, shines anew.

The joy the pleasure, of your smiling face
The touch and feel, of your warm embrace
Whispered words, for me to treasure
Our love I know, will last forever.

Sue Sherriden, Chelmsford, Essex

NOT YOUR TURN

That look on your face when I said goodbye
You forced a smile, I wanted to cry
We both knew the problem, but neither would say
I guess we just hoped it would go away.

We skirted around avoiding to mention
The fact that 'one word' might cause apprehension
It's hovering above just like the grim reaper
Waiting to strike as your pain grows deeper

You look like a child so vulnerable and weak
From your hospital bed the future looks bleak
Cancer's a word, just like so many
I'd gladly replace it, but can't think of any

But all is not lost, so many pull through
With the right treatment, you'll soon feel like new
There's so much to live for, and so much to learn
Don't leave us just yet ma, it's not your turn.

Peter Bridgeman, Kennington, Kent

THE STRENGTH OF LOVE

Love is wonderful
Love is strong
Love is secret
But it could be wrong

You give me your heart
I'll give you mine
I'll wrap you in warmth
And make you find
That all you need
Is my love
To help you go on

Make me strong
And help me to fight
To secure my love
With all my might
Give me courage
And give me faith
To help me go on.

Lorna Charles-Cross, Swanscombe, Kent

Born in Trinidad **Lorna Charles-Cross** enjoys classical
music, reading and playing the piano. "I started writing
poetry 10 years ago," she explained. "I was influenced by
occurrences in my life. My work is influenced by my
lifestyle, my family and friends and my style is heartfelt. I
would like to be remembered as one of the great female
poets." Aged 47 she is a nurse with an ambition to become
a professional poet and to publish books. She has two
daughters and her biggest fantasy is to become the first
black female laureate. She has written over 100 poems
and also several short stories.

UNIQUE

No leaf is as golden as your beauty.
No leaf has an ounce of your charm.
Through Autumn leaves bloom yearly,
And will do so whilever life lasts,
I still prefer the gift of your bounty:
Incomparably more precious, because
more kindly;
Able to give... only once!

Kevin Worsnop, Rochester, Kent

MAN OF THE FOREST

Old man of the forest, you have no home
They've cut down the trees, to furnish our homes.
Nowhere to swing to, nowhere to climb.
No shade to dwell in, when the blazing sun shines.

Old man of the forest, with your
bright orange hair
No forest to live in, so barren and bare.
They put you in cages, they tie you with string
Nowhere to climb to, nowhere to swing.

Chainsaws and axes, they go round in gangs
One less tree for the Orangutan.
Some people out there do really care
for the man of the forest, with the bright orange hair.
If it wasn't for them, you'd be no more
Dead like trees on the forest floor.

Kim Reeves, Southend on Sea, Essex

FOR BERYL, MY MUM

A solitary craft bobbing gently in the morning breeze,
Surrounded by golds of Autumn leaves.
Whilst walking round this lonely path,.
I hear your voice, your gentle laugh.
This was your special hideaway,
Where you would wander every day.
In peace and calm, tranquillity,
I feel that you are close to me, in this your special place by
the sea.
But now you have gone, so far away
and I know that we shall meet again some day.
But here I feel that you are close to me
in this, your special place by the sea.

Christina Palmer, Chelmsford, Essex

*To Beryl Stuart who died 12th September 1997. I love you
and miss you. This one's for you, God bless.*

FATHER

"Where has the time gone". I heard my mother say.
"Has it really been three years since dad passed away".
"Do you go to visit him at the place down the hill"
Do you lay flowers by the tree with daffodils".

She knows it's not always easy, as I work
Throughout the day.
And there's always the weekends when some
Other job gets in the way.
And she'd like to visit him more often
Than she can,
To tell him she still misses him
That brave, clever lovely man.

But maybe this Sunday, an effort I'll make,
I'll pick up my mother and some
Flowers we'll take.
We'll spend a short while so he knows
That we're there,
After all he's my father and always I'll care.

James Parsons, Maidstone, Kent

A SACRED HEART

All of us are brothers and sisters
Born all mortals, children of Jesus,
Open up a pathway of guidance
Put away selfish thoughts
Teach us to give a holy thought
Seek peace to reign
Ever more throughout the land
Helping one another truly understand
One's own worth in life
Learn to live in each day as we pray
What need do we have for the expensive,
Not to compare with worthless wealth
Holy Kingdom in thy treasure palace
Built upon a strong foundation
Covered with blessed happiness
With hearts filled with peace and love inside
Shout "Hallelujah", our praise
Jesus is alive
And lives today, Our Saviour will listen to you as you and I
pray
Take Jesus home in your heart today.

Antoinette Christine Cox, Basildon, Essex

LAST WISHES

Now my time is drawing near,
I want to thank you Sister dear.
For you devoted half your life,
Since the day I lost my wife.

Your kind of woman is so rare,
Your life revolved round my wheelchair.
You cared for me, and my dear Son,
Your days of work were never done.

When I was slowly getting worse,
You were Mother, Sister, Nurse.
I lost the use of arms and legs,
And I could only move my head.

Your kind devotion through the years,
Helped dispel my secret fears,
Now nothings active but my mind,
I'm trying hard for words to find.

For all the things I left unsaid,
That still lie dormant in my head.
If I could say "You eased my pain,"
I could sleep, and never wake again.

Milly Hatcher, Chelmsford, Essex

NOW THAT I'VE FOUND YOU

Alone at night I sit and think and when I'm asleep I dream.
Searching for the perfect love all was lost it seemed.
I wished I hoped and waited for my dream to come true.
And now finally I awake and find my love in you.

For you I would travel the universe and beyond.
For when we are together love is our strength our bond.
At last I've found happiness a happiness long overdue.
For when we are together it will be forever me and you.

So close your eyes my darling and allow sleep to take hold.
For you are deep inside my heart and will never feel the cold.
So fear no more my darling theirs nothing you can do.
Happiness is guaranteed now that I've found you.

Daniel White, Westcliff on Sea, Essex

This poem was written for Miss Sarah Gore, my muse, and my first love.

"I started writing in 1992," said **Daniel White**. "I had an accident which made me disabled, so now I have more time to write. My style is romantic and I would like to be remembered for my poetry." Aged 27 he has an ambition to produce his own book of poems. His hobbies include poetry and computers. "I have written about 50 poems and had eight of them published," he said. "My biggest fantasy is to be rich and famous and I would love to meet a famous film star as I think they do a wonderful job. My worst nightmare is snakes because I am petrified of them."

DOVER REVISITED

Come workman with Dulux emulsion,
do not heed the purists revulsion.
Those cliffs I see are a drab sight.
Take your brush and paint them white.

Those grey gulls that do fly
across the ancient Kentish sky.
They should be a different hue.
Take your brush and paint them blue.

Then old soldier Johnie can go to sleep
his appointment with the Lord to keep
to be buried 'neath his beloved Kent
protected from only disillusionment.

Kenneth Shepherd, Maldon, Essex

ADMIRER

I can see in your eyes that you love her,
It's not the way I wanted it to be.
I know that I cannot change it,
But I can still wish you were here loving me.

It hurts when I see you together,
And it seems you're never apart.
You say you didn't want to hurt me,
But still you've broken my heart.

My friends tell me "forget him",
It's just not that easy to do.
I think about you day and night,
And I know I'll always love you.

Clare Ball, Chartsutton, Maidstone, Kent

DREAM HOLIDAY

No scorching sun
On crowded shore
But snowy peaks
Would please me more -
The Northern Lights
And dazzling heights...
This is my dream.

No swimming bath
With shouting crowd
But mountain path
With birdsong loud
And Northern Lights
And starry nights...
This is my dream.

No choking fume
On traffic-way
But meadow-sweet
And scented hay -
Then Northern Lights
And moonlit nights...
That is my dream.

Betty Blythe, Smarden, Kent

SEASONS TO WISH

A broken dream, like shattered glass,
Surrounding a beautiful flower,
Wilting in the hot Summer sun,
Dying on its own.
A silvery moon covered by grey clouds,
With all its strength, trying to shine through,
Only it's tiny followers compete,
Pierce the black, bleak sky.
An Autumn leaf lying in the street,
Crunching under thunderous feet,
Setting the Winter theme of coldness,
Pleading, trying to be heard.
Wishing on a shooting star,
Throw a penny in a wishing well,
Asking for the future from a teller paid to tell,
Hoping to fall in line with fate, or luck,
Or destiny.

Shareena Eradhun, Bexleyheath, Kent

"I started writing poetry when I was 12 because it was such a good way to express my emotions," **said Shareena Eradhun** who was born in Burton-on-Trent and enjoys writing poetry, short stories and playing the violin. Aged 16 she is a student with an ambition to teach children across the world and to become a famous poet. "The person I would most like to meet is Muhammed Ali because he is an inspiration to so many people and has so much to give." As well as short stories she has written many poems but this is the first time she has had a poem published.

COMPANION

Makes me feel safe.
Peace found in his embrace.
No words needed to communicate.
Beside me through it all -
The travelling, evolving, laughter;
As one, becoming (ever so slightly) wiser.
Silently wiped away life's sweat and tears.
Not a hint of judgement in twenty five years.
Loyalty unsurpassed.
A partnership beautiful and rare -
Between a grown woman and a teddy bear.

Sigrid Marceau, Sittingbourne, Kent

Singrid Marceau, author of "Companion" said: "I have been writing poetry since childhood, to enhance my understanding of the universe around me. Now 26, I live with my boyfriend Jan and six-year-old daughter Jasmine." She works full time as a secretary, and other hobbies include ballroom dancing, slimming and presenting on hospital radio. Singrid has a catalogue of around 70 poems, of which about five have been submitted and accepted for publication in anthologies.

THE TRUTH

The truth can be taken differently
By different people
Without different people who would we be?
We'd be plain
We'd be a bulge of bones
Or maybe to the heart and mind ignorance is kind
Let's accept it, there isn't any comfort in the truth
The truth can hit you at any moment
Then you put an end to dancing, hoping, wishing
You can't ever enter upon it again
No matter how hard you try
It's like a cold metal barrier
Beating you rapidly like a wooden stick
The pain is incredible and painful
You can't get past the barrier
But it doesn't seem to be there
So you scream, letting your pain out,
So the next time the truth hits back remember
The truth can be taken differently
By different people.

Chloe Boswell, Sittingbourne, Kent

In loving memory of Brian Marshall 5-7-69 to 10-5-98.

SHEEP IN WINTER SUNSET

Against the Winter sky
The treetops bleed
In the sun's blush.
Sheep graze the snow,
Trusting its white innocence,
Their shepherd standing near.
They do not argue with
The scheme of things,
Raise not a bleat
Of protest or of fear,
Nor flee the augury above
Of sacrifice to bear.

John Hills, Sittingbourne, Kent

URBAN BLACKBIRD

A blackbird came to drink;
Looked around and, I think,
Decided to stay.
Daylight brought his little mate.
Late into the day they flew,
To- and fro-ing, coming and going.
A length of string, a piece of hay
With which to weave their haven,
A nest; to rest and lay her brood.

Not in leafy wood or tree
Free from city's sound,
But by a wall in urban site
High above the ground.
A blackbird came to drink
And sing; to bring us joy
The joy of Spring.

Lydia Dunn, Ramsgate, Kent

DAWN IS HERE

The morning dew,
On the grass.
The spider's webs
Which sparkles like glass.

The bird's high chatter,
In the blossomed trees.
Flying around,
In a sweet Spring breeze.

The opening flowers,
Encouraged by the sun.
The new born lambs,
Which jump and run.

The sound of the milkman,
Who wakes before dawn.
The sunrise in the sky,
The rabbits on the lawn.

Morning is here,
The night has gone.
The sun will shine,
All day long.

Caroline Candy, Sittingbourne, Kent

WAR TIME

When we were young and in our prime,
We were both called up to do our time.
You went to the ATS,
For me, when the country was in a mess.
When France gave in, we were on our own
Churchill said 'We will fight alone'.
Remember when he made those speeches
And said 'We will fight them on the beaches'.
It was to be a torrid time.
Bombs are dropping; it was wicked crime.
Many homes and lives were lost
It was to be a heavy cost.
Those pilots brave, known as the few,
Showed Goering what they could do.
They beat those Germans, known as The Hun
The Battle Of Britain had been won.
For you and me it was to change our life:
For you, you were to become a wife.
For me, I had become a dad,
Six lost years; it made me mad!

L R Sanders, Margate, Kent

REFLECTIONS

The bathroom mirror's fogged,
I wipe it clear with my hand
Revealing the face, that looks at me,
A woman's face, no longer young,
Though full of possibility;

Not the expectant potential of youth,
Waiting for something to happen,
But a competence, a determination,
The ability to make things happen.
Pushing forty's not so bad!

Gillian Harris, Guildford, Surrey

MY STRONG MAN

My strong man, he saved me
From the darkness of the night
When he reached for my hand in the shadows
And led me to the light.

Then my strong man did rock me
As I drowned within my pain
Then he wiped away the tears
And pulled me home again.
For my strong man would defend me
From the demons in the cave
Then he'd hold me in his arms
And he'd tell me I was brave.
So now I know when I've reached safety
When I can be all that I can
It's when I'm held within the fortress
Of the arms of my strong man.

Cheryl Murray, Whitstable, Kent

FLANDERS FIELDS

Flanders fields,
Flanders Mud.
English bones,
English blood.

They came here in their thousands,
And fought and died.
And all because their generals lied.
And all across the nation tears were shed,
For the life blood of England,
Had been well and truly bled.

Ian Callaway, Thanet, Kent

THE RAT RACE

Time to get up - alarm is calling
Time for work - no more stalling

Rush to get ready - want to stay in bed
Rush to get out - can't I stay home instead

Grab a bite to eat and clean up the mess
Grab clean clothes and get myself dressed

Throw clothes on the kids and pack their things
Throw goodbye kisses and wish I had wings

Into the car and onto the road
Into the traffic jam - get into mode

Arrive at the office feeling battered and torn
Arrive late again - just another Monday morn

Carey Sellwood, Canterbury, Kent

ONE FOR KILROY

When you arrived
Kilroy had gone;
the cliffwalk, unsafe,
fenced off for repair.

The fissuring paths
where Kilroy once walked
abandoned to weeds
forced on through the winter.

Seagulls build nests
in derelict huts
littered by Summer
reclaimed by the sea.

Philip Woodrow, Broadstairs, Kent

GOING TO VOTE?

What does the Parish Council do?
What difference does it make to me and you?
It's just a talking shop, I think.
They have their meeting and go for a drink.

It's not like that, it's really not.
When you look, it does an awful lot.
Street lights and play grounds; pools and seats
All get sorted out when it meets.

Well I don't think I'll bother to vote.
Look at the list, there's no one of note.
Why don't you stand if you could do better?
Don't have the time mate. I'd rather watch footer.

Keith F Lainton, Sittingbourne, Kent

YESTERDAY

Can you imagine a time without "Telly"?
Listening to the wireless drone
Meant putting on an earphone -
Like men from Mars!
Aeroplanes like orange-boxes
Tied together with string;
Only one family in a hundred
Could afford a car;
Indeed we have come far!

Can you, then, picture this era so distant?
No Monty Python, David Frost,
Teeth and glasses without cost,
No welfare state.
Luxury coaches were unheard of;
A charabang trip was our delight -
Big tin bathtub on wheels,
Celluloid windows, canvas hood.
Yet still our life was good.

Can you imagine it? I don't have to;
I can remember it - just!

D G Llewelyn, Sittingbourne, Kent

WHAT ARE WE WORTH?

Lying safe in someone's arms
You know you're safe from harm
People are too busy
In a world that's far from pretty

Society doesn't care for you or me
There's a fine line between fate and destiny
But I believe in the things
That were just meant to be

We are insignificant specks on this earth
But to each other we have a greater worth
Important only to one another
A child, a mother, but more a lover

Together we are closer to our dreams
We can make life as good as it seems
Celebrate achievements, laugh away tears
Above all be positive, chase away your fears.

Sara Ring, Ashford, Kent

LUKEWARM ALREADY

Just when you were longing
For a warm bath, it turns out cold
Like the shouldering of silence.
The tap twisted too far or
Not enough to match demand,
Left alone too long for restoration.

Your fault again, you did not gauge
Its temperature early on and make
Adjustments necessary to survive
The tepid, grey and lifeless water,
Lost the chance of warmth and fragrance,
Not even a friendly bubble disturbed the surface.

Pam Coughlan, Welling, Kent

TEAM WORK

Well, you have got to be joking
It's a bit overcrowded in here.
We will have to get an extension,
Excitement buzzing, what an atmosphere!

Now that everyone's working together,
Gosh, we have run out of space.
For we've now spread across the world,
Our aims to make this a better place.

So the world has joined together,
Let's thank God for progress.
Love, understanding and beauty,
Quality and quantity at its best!

Ann Beard, Dover, Kent

GOSSIPS

I'm glad you came to visit me
Come in sit down I'll make some tea.
We'll talk about this and gossip about that
It's just what I need a jolly good chat.

You know that woman at the end of the street
I'm sure she's having an affair with that Pete,
And the lad who lives at number four
He's in trouble again, yes, with the law.

You see those two women just walking past
Haven't they put on weight? They really are vast,
They're always together seeing what they can see
I sincerely hope they're not talking about me.

Cynthia Dray, New Romney, Kent

Cynthia Dray, author "Gossips" has been composing verse
since childhood but only in the last 15 years has she kept
a record. Said Cynthia: "I like each of my poems to have a
specific theme and a definite last line that ties it all togeth-
er. I and my husband Mick enjoy walking with our border
collie Bonnie and take a great interest in the history and
wildlife of the Romney Marsh where we were both born and
still live. I have also written two short stories, one for chil-
dren, and a ghost story based on a personal experience."

CAPTAIN AHAB OF THANET

From the channel of Sea Road
He navigates, directing the traffic,
A gnome-like personae
With a meandering, maritime gait:
High on his head, perched,
A plastic policeman's helmet,
A heavy torch clutched in left fist.
The legs, intact now,
Captain Ahab crosses Westgate Bay Avenue,
Gesticulating, with foam sea-spraying
Over his chin, into Roxburgh Road and
Starboard into Station Road,
Shorts over track suit bottoms,
He heads for Beano's and muttering, he
Magnified, shouts over a polystyrene cup.
Back on his ambulatory exercise, he charts betwixt
Ship-wrecked motorists and the odd pedestrian.
His shanties are shuttered but his cries unexpunged,
Are strident and salty as he sails away from any old day.

Joy Sheridan, Westgate on Sea, Kent

Born in Plymouth, **Joy Sheridan** enjoys reading, art and knitting. "I started writing poetry when I was 19 and wanted to be a poet," she explained. "I would describe my style as versatile but modern and I would like to be remembered as creating something as lovely as Tennyson's work." Aged 53 she is divorced and the person she would most like to meet is Prince Charles. "I think he is a wonderful, dedicated aid worker," she said. "The person I would most like to be for a day is the poet, Andrew Motion." Joy has written several hundred poems and has had many published. She has also written novels and short stories.

WHITSTABLE

Quaint little old town
Safe harbour
Oysters and sunsets
Whitstable
View over Sheppey
Calm blue sea
Nineteen fifty three
Flood water

Build up new sea wall
Sleep safely
Many years to come
Whitstable
Do not spoil its peace
Sleepy town
Quiet calm atmosphere
Slumber on.

Elizabeth Young, Whitstable, Kent

WITH LOVE TO JOANIE

I stretch my arms to touch you
But find that you're not there.
Places which held your shadows
Are now so cold and bare.
Your warmth and joy are absent.
What once seemed right, seems wrong.
Your departure left me hopeless
With no need to carry on.
But still I have the memories
To help me struggle through;
A mist of love and happiness
Which once surrounded you.

Tanya Stephens, Dartford, Kent

A MOTHER'S LOVE

The stars glimmer on the sandy beach
Is life out there? beyond human reach
Do they really understand this world that they watch
Can they feel the coldness of our empty touch.

This world can be cruel and evil. Love, a word in books?
The heat of hatred hotter than the sun can ever look
Is this the setting for our children, is this what we are?
If not then unbury your head don't leave the door ajar.

When we look around us, there's despair and death
But look into your mother's eyes and see the love you left
The kindest person who will love and care is her alone
No matter where you are in life, with her you have that
warm safe home.

H Rich, Chatham, Kent

MY LOVE FOR YOU

You truly are the love of my life
And I'm so glad that I'm your wife
We pledged our vows together
On calm seas and stormy weather
We've had our share of ups and downs
Through all the smiles and all the frowns
My heart is beating like a drum
Wrapped in your arms I will succumb
You hold me close and keep me safe
Your gentle hands caress my face
You tell me that you love me every day
No one can take that love away
We are bound so strong by trust and love
And a little help from up above
And jealousy there's not a trace
No one on earth can take your place

Jean Godfrey, Chatham, Kent

PARTNER

The look in your eye, the curl in your hair, your body neat,
Without you, my love, I am not complete.
The strength of you, straightness of back,
All combine to give me life and loving I lack.
Where are you now, my love, where shall you be?
How, when, if ever, shall you return to me?
Where has he been? Right under my nose,
With a smile, he wakens me from my repose.
My love is found, he is here, where else should he be
As he gently shakes me awake and says,
"My dear, here's a nice cup of tea."

Patricia Dawson, Eastry, Kent

THE EARLY SIXTIES

I'm thinking back to the sixties
To the times of the rockers and mods
The mods they rode their scooters
And rockers, were motorbike bods!

One just had to be one or the other
That's how it all was in those days
Yes - either or mod or a rocker
Twas quaint - in some funny old ways!

But I was a mod on a Norton
And it really did cause quite a stir
As during the mod/rocker battles
We never knew where we were!

'Whose side are you on'? came the question
'I really don't know - I'm not sure'
'I need to be battling someone
But my loyalties are not very pure!

Yes life was lived in the fast lane
Doing a ton, with wind in your hair
When petrol was 4 bob a gallon
And me and my bike were a pair!
                    Boom - Boom

Mike Phelps, Chatham, Kent

LOOKING AT SIR HUGH CASSON'S PICTURES

A tree, a foam of sea,
A sun dipped down with dignity,
A monolith of mountain height,
A fountain sprinkling in the night,
A nimbus in the misty sky,
A cock that will not Christ deny,
An architecture so supreme,
Carried beside a turbid stream.
We see you and reflect this day;
Your pictures are on grand display-
Brief lines enhanced by crystal colour-
Though we are vapour, they're tomorrow.
Inspired by love and beauty proves
An eddying pool that onward moves.

Nola B Small, Bromley, Kent

BILLY

At times like this I find it so hard
To say what I'm feeling, so I'm writing this card
I can't believe that my Billy has gone
It hurts so much, and it feels so wrong.

There are times in life when something precious is lost
And so great is the grief and the emotional cost
Some will say 'just a dog', yet much more too
He brought such joy to me and to you.

Such a wonderful boy, to lose him seems cruel
I now say goodbye to the best friend of all
And sad though it is that he had to depart,
I'll never forget him, he's still here in my heart.

Sarah Ridge, Cheam, Surrey

STRAIGHT FROM THE HEART

Straight from the heart
Oxygen-packed
We'd gush like a fountain
If the artery cracked

We race to the organs
Propelled by each beat
Deliver our goodness
Then start our retreat

Out on our motorway
Home down our lane
One is an artery
The other a vein

Straight to the heart
Now our errand is run
Our mission accomplished
Our duty is done.

James Critchley, Chislehurst, Kent

LUCY

Lucy with her love for cats and dogs
Hamsters, mice, and slippery frogs.
In her tender way.
Tends her rabbit, with the name of Jay.

Lucy could not afford a horse.
But could buy a gerbil, in due course!
Others at school have such expensive things
But Lucy has a budgie that talks and sings.

Lucy loves to dance and always sing.
And now in her teens.
Accepts life's ever changing scenes.
She smiles, and laughs, that certain way.
In her heart a song each day.

Lucy plays the heartstrings, sweet and mild.
Never change.
My own God child.

Frederick Seymour, Bromley, Kent

A UNIVERSAL JOKE

Who came first, Adam or Eve?
And how did she conceive?
All these questions, are to be asked,
We want questions answered not masked.

Who invented sex? There is no real text.
You practice at this universal treat,
Sometimes, you get hot and overheat.

You grunt and groan, til the conclusion,
When the male of the species, gives his infusion.

Then he rolls off your heaving breast,
It's time to get some rest,

Has he left you high and dry? if he has, you weep and cry.
He thinks with ecstasy and lust,
But you wish for the final thrust.
Your business is unfinished,
His organ though has quite diminished.

It has shrunk to minimal proportion,
Now we continue with much caution.
To try to stir him into action,
We need much more than just a fraction.....

Janice Walpole, Orpington, Kent

As well as writing **Janice Walpole** enjoys oil painting and doing
crosswords. "I started writing poetry as an adult," said Janice
who was born in London. "I am an atheist so I tend to write
about my inability to understand how people can believe in a God.
But also I like to make people laugh." Age 56 she has retired
through ill health but was a personal carer for Bromley council.
She has been married for 36 years to David and they have two
children - Tony and James. She has written hundreds of poems
and had about 12 published. She has also written personal vers-
es for friends birthdays and anniversaries.

WEDDING DAY

A wedding today, there's bustle about
So much to do, the flowers to get out.
The church looks splendid
With bows white and gold
The guests are arriving but none
Of them know
Of the dreams, the dramas of the
Couple they see
Who look at each other so radiantly.

I think back where have the years gone?
There's a tear on my cheek
My mascara has run.
I turn and look at the man I see
Who years ago stood beside me.
We're older now, a lot wiser too
But still manage the words
I love you.

Gwen McRandal, Biggin Hill, Kent

ALWAYS

Dreams of you on a white minibus disturb my snatched
sleep
With one eye on the clock, the other on my tiredness
I wait for you
Tapping on the keys at work
Laughing lunchtimes in other company
My heart is ever tugged in your direction
Silent as the moon swells the tide
And like the beach, I wait for you
Struggling through traffic as if in glue
The newsman tells me I am late so speeding I wait for you
A thousand ways I wait for you
Your eyes your smile your arms
Never fail to bleach attendance into nothing
As if my life to this point has not yet started
And even when the ceremonies are done
And whatever weaves this fabric finds me threadbare
Look up on any night - with stars in my eyes
I wait for you

Paul Redrup, Chatham, Kent

MY LITTLE DALE

The day that you were born
It was my happiest day
You were so very perfect
In every little way

I never got the chance
To ever see you smile
Another thing I couldn't do
Was hold you for a while

I watched you every day
Just hoping you would live
Through the good and bad days
Your strength you then did give

Then one day all of a sudden
Your strength you did lose
You lost your fight to live
All your energy you did use

Now you've gone to Heaven
You're memory still lives on
You will always be with me
Even though you're gone.

Christine Bishop, Bromley, Kent

RETIRING - ME

I'm 60 now - had the pip
Until I got a brand new hip.
61 - mostly fun
Lounging about in the sun.
At 62 I caught the 'flu!
63, dancing with glee
'Cos I have a great new knee.
I'm 64 and I adore
My new fellah - he's 34!
At 65 glad I'm alive
I will survive.
Now 66 and full of twinges but
Still getting out to all the binges
67 - Heaven.
At 68 my plate is full
Hardly home, life's never dull
69, wasting time
Cruising up and down the Rhine.
I'm 70 now .... wow!

Pat Sturgeon, Walmer, Kent

NIGHT

The roadway stood deserted, bare,
Only I was standing there
To see the moon and the light it cast
Along the line of houses, fast
Asleep, as midnight strikes the hour.
Soon, a few short hours away
The sun will supersede the moon
And daylight herald in another day.

Rita Laundon, Morden, Surrey

FOREVER

I want this moment to last forever,
To feed on its comfort and never
Forget the one who set me free
To be what I always knew I could be.
I want to mount it in a frame
For life will never be the same.
To breathe its life-giving air,
To have it where it's always there.
I want to keep it like a treasure
Where its viewing will always give me pleasure.
To return it as a loving token
With all the words that are yet unspoken.
To hold it deep within my heart
For it will always be a part
Of the history that has been made.
To have its memory never fade.
But most of all I want to share
This gift with you for you were there.
For you were there yet did not see,
This blessing that you gave to me.

Nikki Wood, Whitstable, Kent

LAST GOODBYE

Stay a while and listen,
So much I want to say,
The thoughts I've left unspoken
While years have slipped away.
Don't listen to the voices
That say I must sleep,
Just bend a little closer,
My voice is getting weak.
Remember all I tell you,
Last chance to have my say,
For I have no tomorrow,
Only yesterdays.

Geraldine Foy, Horley, Surrey

SLICKER OR PICKER

I'm a city slicker
Living under a wicker
Of country lies
Full of humble pies
I've lost all control
And become a part of their foe
I'm part of the bumpkins
Who hide under pumpkins
And pretend...
They're as pure as silk
When all I could do is puke
With rubbish they throw
All words I don't want to know
I guess I'll go back to the city
Where everything is pretty
Fancy cars and fancy people
Who sit in houses
As high as a steeple

Suzan Gumush, Chislehurst, Kent

ODE TO PEARL

I was there with you today
Though you did not hear me
I had much to say about your life and mine
The way you touched me

Did you sense me
I tried to talk to you
Let you know how I felt
That although the tears refused to fall
I was flooding inside

I might have drowned
But I found myself
Knew you wouldn't want a child
But a man

So though I didn't say goodbye
You know I never left your side
And never will
You saw me through a darker time
And I am grateful still

Cye Thomas, Chatham, Kent

LOVE?

The hands that beat her at night
Are the hands she used to hold
The love that burned so bright
Has now turned icy cold.

The hands that brought her happiness
The laughter kept away the rain
The hands she used to caress
Are the hands that bring her pain.

Why, do they do such things
It really does mystify
Why does a ring not mean a thing
Those vows were really a lie.

Where did it all go wrong
The love that was once so strong
Their love is not worth a song
A miracle it lasted so long.

Bill Stanley, Bromley, Kent

SEARCHING

Chase the rainbow till the end is in sight
Where all that you see are the brightest of lights
Blinded and tired from your wilderness years
Your voyage now is over, no more pain, no more tears
As the mist now is clearing and you focus into view
Standing in the sunlight, the journey's end is you.

Claire Miles, Wallington, Surrey

BLACKBERRY GIRL

See the girl
Pluck blackberries
From tangled Autumn hedgerow.
Fingers snatch through briar,
Drawing prized fruit
To grateful, smiling lips
And oh, she ate deliciously.

Tim Bratton, Ashford, Kent

POWER OF FAITH

How you stand
Mocking me
My aims, and
Slowly dissolving dreams.
The heart tumbles towards the toes,
As your understanding is
So blandly superficial.

How you laugh! O let me weep!
Entangled as we are in this -
A sorrowful state of solemnity.

And how I cry....

Yet You - You are IN CONTROL.
And, as this cruel bemusement melts,
I realise that I am loved,
Loved so purely -
Touching embraced.
As I drown in those tears You send me,
You lift me - up, up, up,
As I worship You.

H Bryant, Chislehurst, Kent

SUMMER DAYS

Soft, silvery sands through my fingers,
Sea shells echo the deep ocean's sigh,
Foam kissed blue waters cascade over shingle,
Still, silent. Rock pools mirror the sky.

Magical moments merge into memories
Fragile as footprints along the sea shore
Where dear, distant days slipped through my fingers,
Like soft, silvery sand, to be savoured no more.

Eirlys Jones, Cranleigh, Surrey

Eirlys Jones is inspired by the beauty of the natural world
and the brevity of human life. she said: "To me, poetry is
the computer where I store all life's pleasurable experiences
and my deepest thoughts - a safe place which still allows
instant access to anyone who cares to read my work. I am
married with two children. My hobbies include reading,
music, gardening and creative writing. I and my husband,
John enjoy foreign travel and visiting stately houses. My
poems display a lyrical quality born of a deep love for the
alliterative poetry of my native Wales."

COLOURS IN MY MIND

Black makes me think of darkness
And that leaves me feeling cold,
White makes me think of purity
And that is beautiful to behold.

Red makes me think of violence
And things that may do me harm,
Green makes me think of rolling meadows
And that leaves me feeling calm.

Blue makes me feel all lonely and sad
Like the strain of a woeful song,
Orange makes me think of bright sunshine
And that leaves me feeling strong.

Yellow makes me think of cowardice
And running away from life,
Pink makes me think of gentle things
Like the touch of a loving wife.

Purple makes me think of royalty
Like a king with a sceptre in his hand,
And of God who made the rainbow
And all of this beauteous land.

Maurice A Smith, Gillingham, Kent

A FISH FOR ME!

When you left I sat and cried I thought a part of me had
died
I new not what I'd said or done to me you were they only
one
We shared so much or so I thought but lessons in life must
be taught
Plenty of fishes in the sea! I hope I'll find a fishy for me.

Mum and Dad were very kind they said a fishy I would find
Mum took out her hanky and dried my tears and said
these were my tender years

Your 1st true love at only nine! let it pass love
and you'll be fine
For when your older wiser to the truest love will come look-
ing for you.

And it did at 22 I felt so blessed for finding you
Now I'm older wrinkled and grey
but funny how memories of lost love's stay
Married now for 50 years time to watch my daughters wipe
away their daughters tears.

Juliette O'Brian, Morden, Surrey

Juliette O'Brian said: "I was born in London and began
writing from as early as I can remember, purely for plea-
sure. I am a housewife with an ambition to be known as a
force to be reckoned with, yet compassionate and fair and a
good mother to my children. I would describe my style as
true to life and down to earth. I would like to be remem-
bered as being honest and not afraid to bare my inner feel-
ings and beliefs. My hobbies include days out with my
young daughter and holidays abroad."

FRENCH MARKET

Sutton high street
Invaded at last.
Straight through the tunnel.
Napoleon
How he'd have laughed
Pate and fromage casseroles too,
Sticks of french bread
Chance to say Palez Vous?
When we think of those years
Boney filled us with dread,
Much better old foes should
Be good friends instead!

P M Mayfield, Sutton, Surrey

COMPLACENT

The sky darkens, the clouds burst,
Pours down rain, the goodness of the earth.

Sitting inside, cosy as can be,
Listening to the sound of the wind through the trees.

On evenings like this, I tend to sob,
I think of those with no home, no job.

I realise just how lucky we are,
four bedroom, a roof and a brand new car.

Cardboard city, it seems so far,
Begging for money, with a broken old jar.

The sky settle, the clouds go way,
I believe tomorrow I'll forget this day.

Katie Farrell, Camberley, Surrey

NIGHT TIME

One thing is certain. Night comes to us all.
It creeps upon us and wraps us round
With its dark cloak. We fall asleep.
Who is happy on their pillow?
Who slumbers peacefully? Who weeps for whom?
You and I are free to dream our dreams.
The prisoner in his cell has different thoughts.
He tosses and turns and dreams of the freedom
He has lost. May the night end soon for him.
The night has many sounds
A Wardrobe creeks. A blind taps.
Cars doors slam. Revellers down the road
Call to each other. 'Good night. sleep well!
A fox barks. The vixen howls her answer.
Will they meet in the darkness and have their own revels?
Above the dark city streets moonlight and starlight
Are swallowed by the light of urban lamps.
But dawn will surely come,
Bringing sunlight and the fresh morning sounds.
That too is certain.

Marian Rutland, Carshalton, Surrey

FULL MOON-MOONLIGHT

He is sitting in the sky,
Ivory glow,
Quizzical expression.
"Are you all right now?"
A cloud scuttles past beneath him,
Still he shines.
"Are you sure?
I was worried you know."
I smile back at him,
He never did leave me,
Hardworking companion,
Angel of the night,
Carrier of sleep and peaceful dreams,
Banishing the sun
And all the fear that daylight brings.
Dark clouds cloak him,
Darkness and shadow,
An empty black sky,
But he is just resting,
A moment passes
And he is awake again,
"My friend",
I smile,
Always

Jane Evans, Camberley, Surrey

THEN THAT FIELD

In which county was that field aslant;
Was it Buckinghamshire, or Surrey?
Then, too, that field's gradual descent
To a country road, quiet as Sunday,
Between its accolade of trees.

Then church bells tolled Sunday away;
An aircraft droned war training,
For headlines grew as black ivy;
A motorcycle ranted in disappearing,
Then at last: 'Come, love, let's gentle the grass.'
So ... no bells or war, but sweet loving
With that buoyant girl at furtherance
Now from this dark accolade of trees.

Herbert Smith, Chertsey, Surrey

A PRISONER AT THE END OF THE OCEAN

I wander through the busy streets,
Through I am a prisoner of silence.
No one seems to notice the chains
That constantly tug at my ankles,
Pulling me back from continuing along my path
All around me are alien people in uniform,
They do not appear to hear my voice
Yet I cry out so loudly.
Sometimes I believe the black clouds understand,
But they are soon stolen away
Past the horizon of light
Far off into another world
Like my ship that used to sail
Upon the never ending ocean
Until it met a storm of reality.

Nikki Law, New Malden, Surrey

CHANGE

They're things in life that never change as seasons come and go,
Birds build their nests with twigs and grass and flowers sprout and grow.
The garden looking drab last month is full of budding blooms,
Colours and scents will fill the air with wonderful perfumes.
These things have happened all through time. unhindered they will thrive
And will go on through years to come if our world can survive.
The only changes come from man, thinking he'll change the scene,
Trees coming down, whole forests gone and fields which were once green.
If only people gave more thought to what they would destroy.
For future generations, for our children to enjoy.
I know some things do have to change, but please in, moderation
Don't spoil the beauty, kill the joy for the next generation.

Joan Cooke, Morden, Surrey

THE VISIT

Its a while since I paid you a visit
I am older, - the journey is long.
But don't think that I have forgotten
My love for you burns, deep and strong.
The rose that I planted has flourished
I chose it because of its name - 'courage'
For on my recollection your hearts
were filled with the same.
"I must clean that stone" its so dirty
No matter, the words stand out clear.
Engraved, etched in forever.
Loving father, loyal wife, mother dear.
Mum, to this place we'd often come walking
You would look at me laugh, and say "Jill
Remember one day I'll be joining your dad
Upon this very same hill,"
So don't think that I have forgotten when
My visits all fade away.
You're not dead - you walk here beside me
Each minute, each hour, every day.

Jillian Hockley, Morden, Surrey

C'EST LA VIE

she tore through my life and left no trace,
I say her name now with a smirk on my face,
She treated me bad, I was naive,
I look back now and it's hard to believe,
That was me being played like a fool,
I thought she was fine, I thought she was cool,
I realise now she's a waste of time,
A little girl with men on her mind,
She wasn't that fit, the sex was crap,
I looked at my life and took a step back,
I realised I'd seen this somewhere before,
With one of my friends who was dating a whore,
Everyone said you can do better,
I gave her chance, I'd only just met her,
They told me to leave her, I could not see,
Blinded by lust, she exploited me,
An experience, it was nothing else,
It could have been worse, I still had my health,
Now it's over, come to an end,
She wasn't a lover, she wasn't a friend.

Michael Robertson, Blindley Heath, Surrey

OVERCAST

Water like crystal falls from a fountain stone
Last week you were there, watching, blending
Into nature, with your faultless, pastels eyes.
What can you see when your gaze falls on water?
A reflection shimmers, but it isn't yours my dear.
You know a girl you can't discard.
I send you wishes when you are standing there,
Just so unkempt and a countenance fading.
Sickly pale, your eyes translucent as the water they
observe.
Oh my dear, clouds gather stealthily
And rain on all but you.

Calm clouds thicken oh carry me to you.
Your splendid lips sip tea regally for you are almost
monarchical.
Unprepossessing-your paradise lost. Or never gained.
Is she really worth it? Is she just as pale?
You know you're worth so much to us. Is she regal too?
Oh my dear, clouds gather furtively
And cry on all but you
Oh you know you're such a funny one to love.

Annabel Kinnear, Camberley, Surrey

IN TRUTH

Roses bring such pleasure
In our gardens as they bloom
Each a velvet treasure
Of sweet and rare perfume.

The fragrant scent of honesty
Scattered where seeds fall
It's silvery trace in winter
A favourite of us all.

No hybrid cultured plant
Addressed by special name
Sweet honesty
Untouched unspoiled by fame

This lowly humble plant
Thought by some as but a weed
Imagine, Honesty, recognised, symbolised
Perfect antidote for greed.

"In truth" might one suppose
Symbolising honesty, the idea grows
Nourishing flourishing, superseding that
Perception, the vision of perfection, a rose.

Mildred Barney, North Cheam, Surrey

TIME

One minute he's hear
And then he's gone
Old father time
Goes marching on.

He never stops night
or day
Sometimes he's bright
Sometimes he's grey
But he never stops
Trudging along life's
Way

What would happen
If he did just stop
We would go spinning off
Just like a top
Into the universe
And become a star
There we would not
Need a car.

Trixie Bolter, Wallington, Surrey

CHANGING SCENE

The landscape was not quite believable
a field of oilseed rape, a paintbox chrome,
a slowly rising copper tinted moon
glowed in a sky still of a startling blue.
Colours like these Van Gogh might well have used.
But we moved on, a green field came in view,
the colours blended and we then could see
sky, moon and field as one harmonious whole.

Alison Lanning, Dorking, Surrey

THE HOPE OF RETURN

S, bring back your sunny smile
that used to greet me everyday.
Make me laugh and make me feel loved,
as you used to, in your special way.
You seemed to have fled from our microcosmic world
which, you used to call our bubble;
Return! come back! our relationship is in trouble.
I need you here beside me and
I think you need me too.
Look into your heart and remember
the meaning of Me and You
We had many good times and many bad,
just like all relationships are supposed to have.
There is no point in getting out because the going
gets tough or the road is too rocky to climb.
It's through those hills and mountains that
I really need to know that you are mine.
There was a spark of love, a little while ago.
Help me to relight our candle into a warm healthy glow.

Montserrat Kidwell, Chessington, Surrey

"I started writing poetry in the late 1980's and my earliest
work was about animals and nature," said **Montserrat
Kidwell** who was born in Epsom. "My work is influenced
by relationships, experiences and my moods and my style
is romantic and philosophical." Aged 25 she is a Spanish,
German and French teacher with an ambition to be a
singer and actress in the West End. She is single and has
an MA honours degree in Spanish, French and German
from the University of St Andrews and a PGCE from
Homerton College, Cambridge. " The people I would most
like to meet are Judy Garland and Frank Sinatra, because
they were such excellent singers," she pointed out. Her
hobbies include singing, acting, dancing and travelling.

NONSUCH PARK

The white lillies blossom in the pond.
The birds build in the trees.
dark pines sway in the breeze.
clear blue sky around me.

The dogs are barking
running across the grass
to chase the seagulls.

People come fly kites
run, play tennis see the sun
have lots of fun,

Children playing hide and seek
cricket, football, fairs and fetes
mansion house and arch way gates.

Field, woods, meadows
places to explore life is never a bore
in nonsuch park.

Valerie Ryan, Cheam, Surrey

Born in Sutton in St Heliers, **Valerie Ryan** enjoys writing, photography and reading. "I started writing poetry in college and realised I was good at putting rhymes together," she pointed out. "My work is influenced by Patience Strong and my style is romantic." Aged 42 she is a factory worker with an ambition to be famous for her poems and have parties with the right people. She is married to Louis and the person she would most like to meet is Cliff Richard. "I like his songs very much," she said. "The person I would most like to be for a day is Marilyn Monroe." Valerie has written many poems and had several published.

HOW MANY TIMES

How many times, have you heard it said,
You can be what you want, it's in your head,
Be forthright and make your aim,
It's the only way, if you want to be in the game.
Keep a clear mind, and go for gold,
Or sit on your arse until you're old,
What's it going to be, which way will you go,
If you don't make up your mind, you'll run out of dough,
So stand up and be counted, and make a plan,
Or throw away your life, and be a wasted man.

John Burstow, New Malden, Surrey

John Burstow, born and raised in Wimbledon, and now living in New Malden, said: "I started writing poetry in 1998, influenced by having cancer in 1991 and the effects it's had on my life since then, and the love of a woman I met in 1992. But sadly nothing came of that. I am divorced with an adult daughter, I am into the arts, drawing, painting, writing short stories, and of course poetry. I was also a film extra for a few years. By profession I was a painter and decorator and market trader. At the moment I am trying to get my life back together, so writing about it seems the best way."

ALONE AGAIN

Alone am I to remember my man
To pick up the pieces as best I can
So kind and gentle he was to me
And always he wanted to be with me
One day we'll meet again
One day we will live again
In another world a beautiful place
He will take my hand
And then embrace
Sleep well my dear
I love you still but
But I'm not there.

Jean Fitzgerald, Wallington, Surrey

SEEING YOU

I thought I saw you, but it was a distant cloud,
Balancing in the sky, a shape not to be scorned.
A voice inside spoke out quite loud,
"For you, I shouldn't have mourned"

I thought I saw you in the distant trees,
Straight and tall, a face in the greenery,
Inside my being flees',
All twisted, like branches, that's me.
I thought I saw you but it was a ship at sea,
Swaying on the waves, I gaze,
I am the lost spirit trying to be happy,
I look for you in the misty haze.

Anna Parkhurst, Richmond, Surrey

LOVE

What is love? Is it butterflies?
Tell the truth now, no more lies.
How does it end? How did it start?
Is it in my head or in my heart?
I don't think I've ever felt this way before,
Turned over a new leaf or at least opened a door.
Oh please let me know,
As I love you so.

You smell as sweet as a flower,
Are you in control, with all the power?
I'll do anything for you,
You do feel the same way too?
Will you please walk out with me,
So the whole world can see,
How kind, sweet and loving you are.

But, will our love go far?

Meri Gadd, Bromley, Kent

MY LOVE FOR YOU THEN AND NOW

I see you on the silver screen,
I know where you go, and where you've been,
You're on my mind and in my eyes
I see you laugh, I hear your cries.

You're in demand everywhere,
You travel by road and in the air,
Life is exciting, so you think,
When you lie back, with a script and drink.

You're in a film I do not know,
In black & white of years ago,
Then young and pretty and in your prime,
With time for all and time to shine.

But now the years have come and gone
And so all the fame as well
They look for new and younger now
With talent and voice to sell.

But wait a while, all said and done,
I love you just the same,
My heart beats stronger now
Because you bear my name.

Ronald Bailey, Guildford, Surrey

OTHER PEOPLE

Study hard a crowded street,
Watch the folk go by.
Spare a moment to peruse
The scene before your eye.
Pause to think and ponder on
The people as they pass
Not just as units in a mass
Distinct by means or class.
For among the living throng
Each mind, each working brain,
Has the power to make and hold,
The right wherein to gain
A life of happiness and peace
In his or her domain.

Jessica Jarlett, Thames Ditton, Surrey

DESERT SUNSET (WESTERN EGYPT)

On the horizon a pylon
Not of the ancient kind
Is silhouetted against a coloured sky
Around it only sand.

The light show of red and orange
Blue and shades of grey
Will soon give way to a silver moon
As night takes over day.

The noise of deadly silence
Is ringing in my ears
Sights and sounds this beautiful
Can reduce a man to tears.

Andrew Fleming, Croydon, Surrey

WHITE VIOLETS

At the foot of the Downs,
In the orchard,
Under the gnarled, ground kissing, branches
of the ancient quince tree,
A patch of white violets glowed translucent
in the moonlight.
I gathered them for you, wishing to share
this moment of magic.
Packing them gently in dew damp, emerald, moss,
I sent them to you with all my love.

You rang to tell me they had died.
You could have lied.

Wendy Lewis, Midhurst, Sussex

Wendy Lewis said: "I was born in Sussex and grew up enjoying the freedom of the countryside, and the neighbouring farm. Educated at Chichester High School for Girls. I went on to a varied career as post office clerk, pub landlady, dog breeder, farmer, freelance journalist and mildly successful poet. Though I can on occasion be serious, most of my writing success has been with humorous articles and short stories read on local radio. My forthcoming novel 'The Reluctant Farmer' will be available next Spring."

THE TOURISTS

The tourist is weighed down with dutiful zeal
and cameras.

If American, several, with light meters and boxes for the
extra reels.
Germans, one, but the most expensive and extensive
Italians are too busy talking, they are not snap happy and
only flash occasionally
As for the Brits with their cines, oh feel for their friends
with after dinner viewing, explanations, events
sensationally exposed.

Hide the boredom in the darkness marked with shapes
upon the screen.
Who proposed
this price for a dinner, steak and chips with frozen peas
and the recurring theme
like the never never
"And there's our guide again, the one with the pink
umbrella.

Teris Vanneck-Surplice, Richmond-upon-Thames, Surrey

LOVE AND PEACE

Our God who resides in heaven above,
Whose son was sent to Earth to teach peace and love
This was many years ago so we were told,
So now it the time to start to unfold,
The mysteries of love and peace,
When wars and killings do not cease
Why oh why, is there so much greed,
Of taking land that other need
The world was given for all to share,
Not for those who do not care.
They kill and maim for other land
This is so hard to understand
Many tears are shed by those who tread
On land they don't know with no where to go
Their homes destroyed by enemies unknown
And there is no mercy shown
The teachings of love and peace
Seem now not to exist
Life was given to enjoy this world
My tale of woe is now unfurled.

Phyllis Elmes, Coulsdon, Surrey

EAST SUSSEX DOWNLAND

Giant, green pillows nestling close to the sea,
Held in check by cliffs of Antarctic white.
Sheep graze and keep watch as their lambs run free,
Larks arise arrow straight, reaching a great height.
On these same slopes Roman soldiers patrolled.
Leaving traces of camps, still to be found,
With pottery shards, coins covered in mould,
Thrown up when the plough goes deep through the ground.
High on the hillside above Litlington,
Rests a white chalk horse, visible for miles.
By the river Cuckmere lies Alfriston,
An historic, picturesque domicile.
East Sussex Downs full of beauty and charm,
They emanate peace and a sense of calm.

Eileen Ward, Seaford, Sussex

Eileen Ward said: "I have been writing for over 20 years
and well over 100 of my poems and stories have been pub-
lished. Many of my poems feature the countryside and the
sea." When not writing, Eileen, enjoys playing her violin
with a group of local musicians.

GHOST

You're the one I loved the most
You visit me, you're a ghost
You seem to know when I'm low
I feel you beside me, there's a glow

I know that from beyond
You still of me are fond
All my secrets with you I share
On different planes, still a special pair.

Sandra Lunnon, Bognor Regis, Sussex

Sandra (Tomsett) Lunnon, was born in Cocking, West Sussex in 1951. Editor of the "Poetic Circle of Friendship," which was founded in 1997. The circle has 95 members worldwide. They have published 22 booklets, linked to different charities, also tapes for the blind. Sandra said: "It's nice to feel that our poetry is being enjoyed whilst helping others." Sandra, published in India by editors, Dr H Tulsi, "Metverse Muse" and Biplab Majumdar, "Voice of Calcutta." Author of "Poetry from Different Planes". For further information contact Sandra Lunnon, 50 Flansham Park, Felpham, Bognor Regis, West Sussex, PO22 6QN.

WHAT A BEAUTIFUL DAY

Sometimes I hop I die,
TO prove that someone cares.
I imagine my funeral pyre,
Will the child I saved last night be there?
Will the couple I smile at each day even care?

I have to read through diary entries
To remind yourself of what I've done in life,
Because no one ever tells me.

I know you're frustrated, you're obsessed with reassurance
But when I tell you how much people love you, you laugh it
off

Sometime I want to die,
To prove that everyone cares.
When they align at my funeral
They will be forced to declare,
That I was a great person,
That will make worth it all.

But you are too much of a coward to end your life,
But you are too much of a coward to be happy with life
And you're dragging me six feet under to,
But I suppose you've never thought to care have you?

Dave Salisbury, Carshalton, Surrey

"GOODBYE."

"Goodbye! dear Sea" I'd stand and say.
"I'll come again another day."
Two lovely weeks of sea and sand;
I'd had such fun; it was so grand;
It might be Margate, Folkestone, Rye;
How sad to have to say "Goodbye!"

Though twenty years have now gone by,
I still recall that sad "Goodbye."
I couldn't tear myself away
Until I'd had that chance to say
"Goodbye! dear sea. I'll soon return,"
And for that day how I did yearn!
I'd say it o'er and o'er again
Until we'd nearly miss our train!
My parents knew just how I felt:
My rueful face their hearts did melt!
But now my promise to the sea
Is in my husband's company,
Except that I no longer say
"Goodbye! dear sea, until that day."

Charmaine Bourton, Croydon, Surrey

Charmaine Bourton is a librarian and is in charge of two small libraries. She is married to Robert and they have twins, Susan and Richard, aged 3. Charmaine has written poems for a hobby since she was a small child and is available to write poems on a commission basis. Please feel free to contact her on 020 8395 9209 for details. In the small amount of free time allowed her by Susan and Richard, Charmaine's other hobbies include drama, reading, travel and some sport.

FRIEND OF YOUTH

Not meeting for so many years
I find it distressing you lay so ill.
Your former self now a shadow
As when we walked and played together.
You were never with the crowd but a singular
Way of knowing how to overthrow
Your problematic childhood. Now still
I see you remember them in tears.

The balding head from chemotherapy
A cylinder of oxygen at the bedside.
I shudder from the breathless voice
Knowing once it was so firm and strong
Wondering why and how long
Time will run it's course. The choice
Is never one for us to decide.
Our talk concerns only days of yesterday.

Derek Betson, Brighton, Sussex

Born in Brighton **Derek Betson** enjoys gardening, singing
and walking. "I started writing poetry in my youth then
wrote more poems at various times of the years," he
explained. "My work is influenced by friends, neighbours
and world affairs and my style is mainly conservative I
would like to be remembered as a singer with a fine voice."
Aged 67 he is a retired with an ambition to sing opera with
the backing of a full orchestra. He is married to
Gwendoline and they have two children and five grandchil-
dren. "I have written many poems but this is the first time
I have had one published," he pointed out. "I have also
written short stories recorded for the Diabetic Association."

DESERTION

Her heart has become like rock
Cold and hard, since he left
the pain she felt
Was as a shard of broken glass
That cut right through and tore her apart
There is nothing left for her now
Just memories of a once happy past.

Her life is a desolate beach
Where waves of loneliness
Run across a deserted shore
Her heart and mind are out of reach
To all around her, evermore.

This wasteland that she lives in
Is full of darkness and despair
There are times she feels she cannot breathe
There isn't any air
She is drowning in her sorrow
Pulling her down to the depths of her soul
She can see no tomorrow, no way out
of her lonely black hole.

Carole Harradence, Sutton, Surrey

SHRINKING

"Hello. Hello...Are you there?
Can you help me?
I'm shrinking.
Yesterday I could reach the top shelf
Today it seems further
than the moon.

Hello? I know you're there
I can hear you breathing.
I'm going to be trodden on
without your help
or washed away in the rain.
No one else sees me shrinking
I know you do.
Hello? Hello?...."

Catherine Simmons, Morden, Surrey

NIGHT OF THE FULL MOON

On this planet we tilt and sway
In a different kind of way
One day the earth might stop
Then we might start to mope.

Improving the earth to keep it safe
Before it might turn to waste
The ozone layer is getting thinner
People on earth are getting dimmer.

War is born, peace is dead
Greed and hunger are being fed
Bad has won good has lost
Losing its battle in a deadly frost.

Patricia Hassett, Mitcham, Surrey

ROMANCE

I'll tell you of the feeling
When love is in the air
Of eyes enhancing pleasure
And courage more to dare
I'll show you secret glances
When eyes do contact make
The touches and the nearness
And hobbies that you fake
I'll tell you of the newness
In what is said and done
The easy going talking
When all is bright and fun
Tell me to heed my reason
And question what I hear
But, no I just won't listen
For now I have no fear
Enjoy this time of wonder
Of happiness and joy
Long may it last and flourish
Such moments can be rare.

Hilary Ingle, Normandy, Surrey

MY DAD

Oh dad you are a good man,
You wouldn't hurt a fly,
Hardworking, uncomplaining,
A thoroughly, pleasant guy,
You worked such long, long hours,
Your wages were not good,
You sacrificed so much for us,
To give us what you could,
Oh dad you never smoke or drink,
I've never heard you shout,
You've never ever raised a hand,
To smack us kids about,
You're really so obliging,
You answer any call,
To help out friend or family,
No task too big or small,
Oh dad I've never told you,
The things that you should know,
How much I truly love you,
And appreciate you so.

Christine Brown, Morden, Surrey

MY GARDEN

I sit in my garden and shut my eyes
No doubt there are a few harmless flies.
In my garden is a paradise view
Roses old and some are new.

Birds are singing and lovely to hear
My dog chases the cats when they come near.
Aeroplanes noises fade, they fly through the air
Grey collared doves, land in a pair.

Grey squirrels approach, what a gratifying sight
The day draws nigh, a red sky at night.
I love my garden with nature buzzing around
Spiky hedgehog, our dog has found.

My husband's energy has gone into a colourful view
Red admiral butterflies, I can count a few.
Days in the summer can be very hot
Birds drink water from a garden pot.

As I write this poem two magpies have flown by
Assortment of birds, seagulls and flies.
The sun will go down, will sprinkle our array
Everything will be the same, the very next day.

Beryl Coles, Shoreham By Sea, Sussex

INSANITY

They are dropping bombs on a country,
Raining death down from the air,
Have we not learnt any lessons,
There are people way down there.

A bomb cannot recognise,
If you are friend or foe,
So stop this bloody lunacy,
And give diplomacy another go.

We will make our world a graveyard,
Millions of crosses point to the skies,
Pause now and think, before it's too late,
Before one other person dies.

Terry Sorby, Hastings, Sussex

THE HOSPITAL CHAPEL

With her face averted from
The stranger's gaze
She sat so still in the
hospital chapel.

Sad heavy thoughts
Bowed her shoulders down
Dark tired hair hid
Her cheek.

Now she lifts a hand
To brush her cheek,
Did a tear fall there?
Dear God, I hope not!

Michael Rowson, Chichester, Sussex

FIRST WORDS

This will be my first sentence
and I don't think
there will be any fanfares
the sun won't appear
miraculously
nor the cloud clear
to reveal the heavens calling
but somewhere, maybe here
or on the fare eastern tip
of a western land
in the southern hemisphere
the sea will drown in the sand
and an old man sitting motionless
will tap his feet
to the sound of this
my first sentence.

Joanna Skelt, Hastings, Sussex

DOG TRAINING

I am a little German Spitz,
Full of life and one year old;
My mistress takes me to weekly classes
To teach me to do what I am told.

Sit on command; come when I'm called;
To hear them shouting you'd be appalled;
Walk to heel, that's what I like best,
Then going home and having a rest.

My mistress is exhausted too,
Though I don't know why, she had nothing to do.
As she sips her tea she murmurs 'well
That was an hour of purest hell!

Me and my chums, we all agree
That it's the adults we'd like to see
Put through their paces to see if they
Could improve their behaviour in any way!

Mary Mumford, Rowfant, Sussex

MOUNTAINS

The dark mountains of Scotland, so beautiful to see
Surrounded by their swirling mists
Have captivated me.

With their tall majestic splendour, rising from the sea,
With patchwork clouds of many hues
So white and soft and free

They stand like guardians of the loch
So quiet, so dark, so serene,
And their overwhelming presence enfolds you as in a
dream.

They stand regal and magnificent by the waters of the loch,
Where the ferries turn, the yachts drift by,
And eiders gather in a flock.

My dream is that I will return to those mountains very
soon, To that tranquil place beside the loch
To the place that's called 'Dunoon'

Jan Imeson, Burgess Hill, Sussex

UNDECIDED UNDERLING

The undecided underling (who hails from the Rann of
Kutch,)
Sat whimsically wondering (and wandering as such)
Preposterously pondering too far (and far too much)
On all the things that dwell far off (too far away to touch.)

The undecided underling was on a jolly journey
Into the
Land of Everythingtoolateandmuchtooearly
And passing through the forest where you cannot see too
clearly
The trees refuse to shed their leaves (they love them far too
dearly.)

The undecided underling lived deep inside the mind
of an undecided overling who'd left his self behind
in the Land of Longandlostandgone which nobody could
find
where the sun that no one ever saw sat sleepily and
shined.

The undecided underling could never really stop
his trip to upper yesteryear until he hit the top
Where the Bubble of Eternity sat on the pin of pop
And the sun that no one ever saw shut up her shiny shop.

AJK Herbert, Brighton, Sussex

SAYING SORRY

The hardest thing sometimes to do
Is saying sorry to folk around you,
Especially the ones we love so dear
To swallow our pride, and find good cheer.
Bury the hatchet, smile once more,
Try to be kind, not cause a war!
It takes a big man to admit he;s wrong
But you will find it pays before very long!
Don't shout about or lose your temper,
But ask the other one just to remember
The good times you had when you were friends!
And always try to make amends,
Folk have to sit, talk things out, not to shout!
Talk all the differences you feel wrong
Try to "give and take," it will pay off before very long
Start again, talk out problems, but on each side.
Seeing other views, no need to hurry!
You'll be pleased that at least you tried!
For life's too short to be unkind, and
We have but "awhile so bear that in mind!!"

Jean Walker, Brighton, Sussex

MOONLIGHT BATHING

The waxing moon pulls the lax body of the sea,
rivulets on the newborn shore
rejoin their source
as sliding silver serpents
meet a fringe of foam.
Breezes stroke the waters
undulating like a cat to the caress.

Two bodies break the silky skin,
white bodies shimmering in the moonlight.
They play, embracing in the buoyant waters,
like spirits released from substance and gravity,
like seals having lumbered from the shore.
As air meets water they scarcely know
they have bridged the elements.
A primordial scene, and old perceptions
which rise in dormant memory.

Betty Blum, Worthing, Sussex

THE DARKNESS OF STRANGERS

The darkness of strangers is something unique.
Not the darkness that hangs in a room without light,
Nor the darkness of sky on a cold winters night,
But of the unknown, darkness steeped in
mystique.

It swallows you up with a sense of unease.
A simple release: just a question, remark,
From a head full of light to a head full of dark,
And the search beam is on for a moment to seize.

But there's always a point where the shutter will fall.
When the lights flooding through and discomfort aside,
There's always a corner the darkness can hide,
Yet a warm glow is often enough for us all.

Georgina Harris, Haywards Heath, Sussex

REMEMBER

Remember the times, we would talk all night.
Remember those times, we would put the world right.
Remember the times, you would help me undress.
Remember those times, we'd make love then caress.
Remember the times, we would long for each other.
Remember those times, we were friend's not just lovers.
Remember the times, we didn't notice the rain.
Remember those times, we felt each other's pain.
Remember the times, we thought together forever.
Remember those times, we thought us strangers?
No never.
I remember those times, they are etched on my soul.
Now I feel them slipping away, memories growing cold.
I remember those times we felt we'd come home.
Now I feel I am me, you are you, we are together alone.

Patricia Haffenden, Eastbourne, Sussex

THE SMILE ON HER FACE SAID IT ALL

She was a beautiful lady, Connie was her name
Tall, upright and fair
With love in her heart for all folk
A love she was willing to share
And the smile on her face said it all.

She was a beautiful lady, as everyone would declare
With a helping hand for those in need
It was her nature to care
And the smile on her face said it all.

She was a beautiful lady
With love of natures pleasures,
Pink roses were her favourite
And violets around her home
With the sound of music that completed her joy.
And the smile on her face said it all.

She was proud of her man and loving family,
And suffered illness without complaint,
For that was the nature we all knew,
And when she died, unfairly we thought.
The smile on her face said it all.

Edward Featherstone, Hailsham, Sussex

TIME FOR CHANGE

Time for change, must think of moving
But how difficult it's proving
Looked around my home of many years
But now is not the time for tears
My garden, how I'll miss you
Bathed in sun or clad in snow
Each season bringing pleasure
Each flower, shrub, each pot and tub
How I'll miss you but you, once more
Should have your swing
And with children's voices ring
Have now moved in to my new flat
It has central heating, never had that
Much to do, lots to explore
Wonder who lives in the flat next door?
Time for change, a daunting thought
But to me, new life it's brought.

Iris Owen, Eastbourne, Sussex

THE FIRE

This comes to you straight from my heart,
And I will begin at the start.
I asked for their help they knew I needed it,
But, they didn't seem to care one little bit.
I told them that my heart's desire,
Was to set myself on fire.
They didn't listen, they didn't care,
They just thought that I wouldn't dare!
But I did eight months ago
And still they don't want to know.
Now they've taken my children away
And I get more depressed every day.
My children hate it all you know,
They don't understand why they had to go,
They seemed to think I wouldn't care,
But I can't live without my children there.
My children mean the world to me,
I wish these people could just see.
We have a lot of love for each other,
So why were they taken from their mother?

Tracy Verrall, Brighton, Sussex

FAITH

It is in the grace of God that we are friends.....
In his grace we shall stay that way.....
For nothing more and for nothing less than just friends.
But those innocently floating in the illusion of love can neither live without this element.
Dear friend
You have become this important element in life,
Seeing through those eyes, there is the love and devotion within you.
The loving and caring nature - one of the few qualities that many have not been able to share.
It is in the grace of God that we are friends....
The days of our lived thoughtlessly seem to pass by.
But let this friendship remain unchanged,
Embedded in heart of the heartless.
You will never know for all the tears I cried through the fear of losing you.
With respect I will threat you for nothing more or for nothing less than a friend.
In the grace of God we shall stay that way....

Amardeep Kaur Padam, Colindale, London

ARRIVAL

Not a single thought, no pain, no worry
And no need to think, panic or hurry.
Floating in the water, long lazy days,
No one telling me, to mend my ways.
Not seeking food, constantly supplied,
Haven't yet laughed, haven't yet cried.
Alive, but with no idea what to expect,
I'm vacant, without so much as a dialect.
Waiting to be fed, much more than foods,
Waiting to experience, good and bad moods.
Proverbial empty vessel, waiting for the chance,
To be filled to the brim, dance the human dance.
Almost nine months, fighting hard for survival,
Now screaming loudly, at my moment of arrival.

Danny Coleman, Eastbourne, Sussex

IN DEEP DARK CAIRNS

In deep dark cairns
Under bright green sods
On stone cold biers
Our ancestors slumber
Sightlessly gazing the centuries
In dark grey tombs
Of mud daubed walls
On rock hard beds
Scattered, tumbled, bones lie silent
Students, belly crawl
Along sludge-wet passages
Stand upright, peer torch lit gloom,
Squint at Neolithic skeletons,
People once
Science reveals, diet, occupations, lifespan
But no words tell, of fears, thoughts, dreams
They too are locked
Within chambered vaults
Under bright green sods
In deep dark cairns

June Fox, Orpington, Kent

FLOWN

The lane is strangely still today
No martins cleave the air,
Or dip away from serried ranks
That massed the cables there.

A misted hush hangs over all
Damp leaves drift softly past
And plovers forage in the fields
Where swallows swept the grass.

Barbara Masters, Sevenoaks, Kent

LETTING GO

Don't look at me because I'm crying,
Trying to hide it more and more,
I shut my eyes and now I'm flying
To a place where I've never been before.

Caught up in this world of illusion,
What if I would stay in this land?
I'm ignoring the tears and confusion
And waiting for the touch of your hand.

So don't wake me if I'm dreaming,
Because you know I'm dreaming of you,
But hold me when I'm screaming,
Because you know that its true,
I'm here because you're with me,
You make my world complete
Forever is as far as I can see,
Even if it's only in my sleep.

Don't tell me that it's all dying,
Because I already Know.
So just let me fly forever
It's the only way I can let go.

Racheline Benveniste, Lingfield, Sussex

SERENITY

In undulation, I can move like an ocean wave in the sky,
In recoil to melodious sights.
With wings spread like the sonorous of day.
I can witness the beauty of an illustrious ambience.
I will nurture its stream,
Held within a serene breeze.

I have abandoned Earth to persevere with his voyage.
An evolution into brighter, fragrant future.
One, non existent of humanities antipathy towards their
Elysian field.

Within this actuality,
I will whisper my valedictions to the bleak, barren
residence of my relative
Organisms.
Farewell Children of the Earth.

Heavens energies align, I will admire her refinement.
A soul search of ancient times.
An evenly balanced tranquillity,
Allowing me to be one with equanimity.
Departed from Mother Natures recline.

A refulgent omnipresence, now mine....

Darren Mayes, Morden, Surrey

OLD DAYS

Drink up for the night is young
for we can be merry and be as one.

Your is a gift to give and share
to dance the fields like a mare

Life was once good and still could.
seeing is believing I told you you would

Blink and your miss.

The magical ride on a wave of laughter
with your one and very own master.

Suzannah McCready, Camberley, Surrey

SLEEPLESS NIGHT

I'm tired, I yawn,
Will probably see in the dawn,
Sleep doesn't always come,
Until the rising of the sun,
Tossing and turning,
What will fulfil my yearning?
For sleep! please, body be kind,
Delete all thoughts from my mind,
I suppose it happens when I am stressed
But I'd rather be restless when I'm dressed
Good thoughts, bad dreams intertwine,
Annoyance does seem to be mine ,
My one real chance of relaxation,
Losing out to all the nation,
So in the morning I'm the one
Whose 'not all there' in the sun,
Because I have suffered a sleepless night,
Something we can never fight.

Lauren John, Chelmsford, Essex

GODS GIFT

Was the night quite cold and bright,
Were hill so white with snow,
When the sky with heavenly light
Was lit so long ago?

Shepherds heard the angels bring
Good news -a Saviour's birth,
Joy so great from heavens King
And peace for men of earth.

O that many more might know
That gentle Saviours love,
Come to Jesus, trust Him so,
Then live with Him above.

Anne Charman, Wallington, Surrey

SWIMMING IN DESIRE

A heady scent of lust engulfs
A humming car; a laugh;a shout
danger surrounds. Excitement.
Forbidden explicit knowledge trailing
your body with fresh sweat

F' me eyes and searching limbs
Suicidal plunging
Intoxicating frenzied desire
Muscles hardening under cautious caresses
Undulating pleasure

Fluorescent flickering light
Convincing cries
Devouring flesh with a tongue
Imperfections adrift in an ocean of desire.

Nicola Rudland, Bagshot, Surrey

KATE

A volcanic eruption, a balloon blowing up.
An atomic explosion or a bomb in a cup.
Not one of these can surely compare,
With my sister Kate, when she flies in the air.

Don't think for a moment that you will win,
When like a tornado Kate blows in.
There is no armour against her attack,
If you shove her out, she's sure to comeback.

Her outrageous behaviour and way out ideas,
Will set you squirming and reduce you to tears.
You feel so confused, a shattered wreck,
As her voice gets louder, Oh what the heck!

Your head in a spin, your world falls apart,
When will she finish how did she start?
Was it me? was it you? I really don't know.
Don't panic! sit tight! Sister Kate's having a go.

Jeanne McIntyre, Southend on Sea, Essex

X PART 2

If I had the most exquisite dream I've ever dreamt, it is you, (as you now appear to me when I am conscious.)

If had an unlimited supply of paper, and a pen that never ran dry, it would be impossible to write enough words to describe you... Your innumerable, beauteous facets that cannot fit within an infinite period of time, (constructed sapphires)

If I were a poet, I would hope that one day, you would enjoy reading my words (dedicated) to you... and delighting only to find tears of laughter falling from your delicate, sweet face.

Thank you Jesus, for sending us such a wonderful person in "X"... you made us a treasure to share.

We are overjoyed to have met one of your angels: "X" has spread her wings of love, to make our hearts flutter with your tranquillity.

If I ever meet another woman who had your looks, etc, she wouldn't have your (unique) soul. She would never be a close 2nd, 3rd... or a trillion, to you.

"X", you have such a beautiful heart that, I want to tell the world about it.
What do (your finer) points make?: prize-zest (for life).
"X", (not money) grows on trees (of life and knowledge)
"X" spells... loveliness, pure spirit, heart, Spring days (and daze) in my emotions.

Logan Naidoo, London

SUMMER

The sun comes up long before you and me
Another hot day for us by the sea
The water's warm and so is the sand
A walk on the cliffs hand in hand

Barbeques drinks funfair times
Mine's a lager with lime
Fireworks tonight for you and me
The sun melts down into the boiling sea

Summer's here and we all feel good
Not cold no flu but like new wood
We could dance and walk and talk all night
And watch the sun come up tonight

What a perfect season oh perhaps not so
I wish those wasps and bugs would go
Still it's the best we've got
Even with thunder and rain
So don't be British and don't complain.

Phil Armand, South Woodham-Ferrers, Essex

KISS

When I kissed you
In an arid waste of that cheek
The tangle of your hair did dissect
Indulged in making a tale brief
Of some sombre trivial demise
Of hope forlorn or of rainy nights
And the communications between two hearts
Flowered perhaps in meadows of grass
Sweet whispers stopped not
A song of soul on warm lips
Neither charm away nor stop now
The wonder of love in mind's crypts.

Durlabh Singh, London

MCNICHOLAS MAN

Feeling the curve and swerve
Of the tube train,
Opposite sits
A brutal beauty:
Eyes-chocolate, plain,
Lashes unlawfully long,
Lips; succulent,
Slightly truculent,
Nose; Roman-strong;
Hair-Mediterranean-sleek
(Silver-peppered)
In 'Four Greek
Plays' absorbed,
Unaware I stalk you like a leopard.
I burrow into your furrow
In insistent awe,
Lost in the field of hairs
On the wrist of this
Builder's broad paw.

Les Swain, Islington, London

THE BADGE

It don't bother me, that I won't be able,
To sit with the guests, as they eat round the table,
But I've made a badge, so they can remember,
It's my birthday on Friday and I don't want a jumper,
It's nearly time for bed and they've just started drinking,
Good time for the guests to know what I'm thinking,
A cough out aloud, turns attention my way,
"Look at my badge everybody, I've something to say,
No clothes please, just toys" The message is read
Goodnight everybody I'm going to bed.

Paul Klatsa, Southgate, London

HOLD ON - JULIETTE SEEL

I can be strong, strong without you
You can't hurt me no more
You betrayed me, so I'm leaving
Heading straight for the door
Don't be mistaken, cos I've thought it over,
I've found the courage I need.

Gotta be strong, gotta be strong
Gotta hold on
This time I'm living my life for me.

I see clearly now, all the lies you told,
Were you ever truthful to me
You were my dream, but now it's broken
I know this time, I'm not wrong
It's all over now there's no going back
You've committed your last sin to me.

Juliette Seel, Morden, Surrey

THE BOATING LAKE

The geese sailed by like galleons
Across the boating lake.
Behind them, gulls bobbed up and down,
Cups and saucers in their wake.

A lonely heron watched the scene
On floating island, dumb,
No boaters venturing out today,
The ticket-seller's glum.

I cycled by and 'spotted' birds,
Three mallards and a swan,
"I thought they went around in pairs,
Why is there only one?"

A single child was throwing bread,
White slices, one by one.
Poor birds, they all will be so ill
With in-de-gest-ion.

I parked my bike and sat and watched
This peaceful winter scene,
Then peddled home and left the birds
To stand and float and dream.

Judith Brierley, Ealing, London

IMAGINARY FRIEND

Why could I see you when no one else would
Why could I hear you when no one else could
Why could I tell you my secrets and fears
And know I'd be talking to listening ears
Although you are different, weird and strange
You are my friend and nothing will change.

Meera Patel, Harrow, Middlesex

WHAT DOES LOVE MEAN?

What does love mean?
What does love do?
What is love?
Does love help at all?

Love makes the world go round.
It brings people together
A feeling you cannot explain
It helps you realise the meaning of life.

Love means, well nothing.
Love breaks your heart no matter what.
Love sucks, you know what I mean.
Love helps you commit suicide.

Are the answers meaningful?
Or are they plain cynical?
Love could be anything-think of graphics
How they change shape, make you think differently about
things.
Have a guess, after all.
It's your opinion, not mine.

Tara Brown, Perivale, London

MEMORIES

I was cleaning my teeth,
And whilst I was flossing,
I remembered my pet Dalmatian,
Which I lost on a zebra crossing,

But I didn't mind losing him.
Why? well you know my pet hate:
Dog picking his nose:
I think it's a terrible trait.

Then I remembered the police station,
One thought and I was back there,
I remembered my brush with the law,
When I combed a sergeant's hair.

I was arrested for selling
A fake eighteenth century light in the wet,
I told the undercover cop batteries weren't included;
They hadn't been invented yet!

Clive Perilly, Stanmore, Middlesex

MIRRORED LIFE

In a Springtime when I looked I saw
A baby crawling on the floor
In Summertime a teenage girl
Who thought that she could change the world
Autumn's image showed to me
A woman of maturity
Then Winter came the image died
Swallowed up by human pride
In aftermath of death I saw
New life crawling on the floor.

Bonita Hall, Loughton, Essex

ONE

Because of you I seem to know
How to rearrange and grow.
Because of you I'm real.
Can touch and move and feel.
Because of you I now fly.
Never asking when or why.
Because of you I'm pure and whole,
But sharing in one heart, one soul.
Because of you I'm here.
Have lost the memory of fear.
Because of you I care,
In all the passion that we share.
Because of you I'm one.
Merge with earth and moon and sun.
Because of you I shine.
You most valuable are mine.
Because of you I run and win,
and where you end, I begin.
Because of you, I look and see.
I am you and you are me.

Rebecca Roper, Eltham, London

LIFE

When storms have washed my dreams away
And the winds blown devastation through my mind.
The sun's compassion will melt the snow and
In the sky a rainbow will shine.

Stewart Phillippo, Edmonton, London

THE LOTTERY DREAM

Oh, to win the lottery would be great,
I would say goodbye to my grumpy old mate
I'd be off on a long, long cruise
But I'm diabetic, so not too much booze
But I would be sure every night to have a date
But I can only wish and dream
For riches like Wimbledon's strawberries and cream
and there are so many around just like me
Saying "why can't we win the flipping lottery."

Ethel Stukins, Chelmsford, Essex

POPPIES

I'd wondered why the old lady grew
poppies in her garden.
Such flimsy flowers
like tissue waste,
untidy, ethereal,
soon gone.
She'd smiled and said he'd been like that.
She visited France that year
to tidy him up.
Time had stood still so long.

Ron Woollard, Chessington, Surrey

SLATE

In the long measure of your lungs
stole a beauty, right out of town.
It left you breathless in my smoky air.
But I still had the sense to raise a glass
and take sips with purple prose
about the growing pain of
damaged fairytales and the state of dirty tubes.

In the darkness between out hours,
the slate is being wiped clean.

Jamie Spracklen, Hadleigh, Essex

SPEECH LESS

Trapped in this prison
Who people can't see.
Life goes on around
But on the periphery me.

Silent and entombed in neglect.
Laughter and love working for some.
Freedom and friendship too far out of reach.
Day into day and life never comes.

People are kind, people are cruel.
Coming and going, no regular face.
No one thinks to ask me if
I want to be in this place.

Lynda Daniells, Tiptree, Essex

PHOTO DOCUMENTS 1940: FIGHTER PILOTS RESTING ON ALERT

Too fledgling to take to air
barely out of teens perhaps not that....

Muffled in sheepskin
tousled heads resting on folded arms.
Stripped of bravado
their vulnerability exposed in sleep.

Soon to kill dispassionately, or
fall as Icarus wings melted
on a funeral pyre,

these boys, not yet men
who shoulder death on silver wings,
perhaps remembering in their dreams
those they've left behind
before madness takes their breath away.

Barbara Crupi, Colchester, Essex

BELOVED

If only I could hold you once again,
I would cradle you so close, so tenderly
within my arms. And as I wrapped you warm
in my embrace, our sweet, enraptured storm
of tears would run in rivulets of joy,
to wash away the anger and the pain.

If only you would tell me you forgive,
and that you'll always love me just the same,
I would lift my fallen spirit from the dust,
and everything between us will be just
as it used to be before the sorrow came,
when life was love and love was still alive.

Steve J Waterfield, Rainham, Essex

LIGHTS ACROSS THE BAY

Lights from distant places glitter,
Twinkling from across the bay.
Blurred reflections on the water
Form an epitaph to day.

High above are stars suspended
In those ever darkening skies,
Adding to that air of wonder,
Secret symbols of the wise.

Far-off sails have changed to fireflies
Skimming o'er the dusky sea.
Near at hand that ocean liner
Turns into a festive tree.

Towns of which we see so little,
Towns that fade with morning light,
Spring to life as shadows deepen
Marking the approach of night.

Sidney Morleigh, Islington, London

THE CHRISTMAS CARD

The still is deafening, paralysing, numbing
It rips the heart from the Christmas humming
I see no light, no air I smell
The leafless trees, I cannot feel well
No time like the present to think of the past
Oh angel beside me I hope it's our last
This feeling "alone" I simply can't bear
The world all around me don't love or don't care

This pen confiscates me it leaves me all scarred
Oh what can be done with old Xmas cards

Jacqueline McNamara, Hanwell, London

SOLIDIFY

Bored and frustrated
It seems no one is around
I'm in 'that kind of mood
And I will not make a sound

Publication or imagination
Can both fulfil my desires
The journey is better than the arrival
And then all interest expires

Rise up, solidify
A time lapse flower coming into bloom
This hardening euphoria is now set
The journey will be over soon

The voyeur in me won't look away
I go back and fourth no more
As I put my thoughts to paper
Another fantasy has been explored.

Malcolm Carelse, Wallington, Surrey

YOU MOVE IN YOUR CURVE

You move in your curve
Like the sun's day long route
Now settling into purple trees,
The heat withdrawn into
The pewter shades of evening.
A silence sifts the valley
Where I know the water calls
But does not reach my ears.
I can sense the leaves curl
Into warm lingering browns,
Luxurious in the season.

The high ridge brings sunset earlier,
But that only means more time to live
The subtler meetings of the night.

Alan Chambers, Ealing, London